A View from the Back of the Candy Store

A View from the
Back of the Candy Store

KEN WHITE

Pen & Publish
Saint Louis, Missouri

Published by Pen & Publish, LLC, USA

www.PenandPublish.com
info@PenandPublish.com

Saint Louis, Missouri
(314) 827-6567

ISBN: 978-1-941799-79-6
Library of Congress Control Number: 2020903959

Printed on acid-free paper.

Contents

Dedications

This book came about as a result of the hilariously funny and fascinating things that have happened in my life. It is a compilation of short stories and tales from the back of my dad's candy store to an ashram in India, a souk in Morocco, the streets of Paris, and beyond. The fun and the miracles keep on happening.

You might be staring at a blank page had it not been for my dearest friend and mentor Anna May Sims. It is her encouragement and vision of what is possible that moved me to carry on and keep writing.

My niece Andrea lovingly told her daughter when she was very young, "May you have many mothers in your life," and so I dedicate this book of stories to the many women in my life that have loved, supported, and mentored me. You all have left an imprint on my heart.

Anna May Sims
Jennifer Andrews
Evelyn Silvers
My niece, Andrea Carvin
My sister, Marlene Legatt
Louise Epps
Nancy Shapiro
Cindi Olsman

To my mother who gave me the "grist for the mill," so useful and necessary to create this life that I love so much.

A profound thanks to my writing critique group: Steve Schullo, Lily Berman, Judi Hollis, Genevieve Stokes, and Judith Lieber, and to Professor Chet Kozlowsky, my first writing coach, for his expert guidance and encouragement. To Ginny Weissman for her reassurance and to Kurt Wendelborg for his friendship and technical support.

"In a sense, as we are creative beings, our lives become our work of art."
—Julia Cameron, The Artist's Way

Whitey's Honor Roll

The Japanese attacked Pearl Harbor on December 7, 1941.
I was only a year and a half old and had little comprehension of what was going on, but I was told that Dad's candy store became information central for the goings-on overseas. Each newspaper delivery was a highly anticipated event.

Whitey, as my dad was affectionately called, created an "honor roll" that he crudely constructed out of cardboard with an American flag and a bald eagle at the very top. The names of all the neighborhood boys in the armed forces were posted with their branch of service, where they were stationed, what ships they were on, and where they were deployed. My mother would later tell me of the pride and emotion my dad felt with each hand-lettered entry.

The guys would write my dad, telling him what was *really* going on overseas, and then write a briefer, less worrisome letter to their families. He had a profound bond with them that continued after the war.

Dad also kept track of all the men and woman who were serving and volunteering in factories on the home front. At that time, Americans were very patriotic and pulled together for the war effort by working in factories and sacrificing comforts at home. I remember food rationing and the scarcity of items like meat, sugar, cigarettes, and candy. Automobiles were no longer being manufactured, nor were nylon stockings.

Dad wanted to be involved and do his part, as so many men and women sacrificed their lives and went overseas. He decided to work in a defense plant as a riveter and left my mother to run the candy store. She was not happy about being left with two young children as well as the arduous job of running a store. It was the source of much arguing and tension between them and only added to the stressful time of the war.

On August 15, 1945, the Japanese surrendered. I recall seeing the oversized headlines in the newspaper and everyone hugging and kissing and jumping up and down with joy. The celebration marked the end of World War II and the great anticipation of our troops coming home.

In 1947, my dad sold the candy store, and we moved to Brooklyn to live with my grandparents.

Some of the neighborhood guys on Whitey's honor roll

Old Man Levy's Wife

In 1952, after living with my grandparents for five stress-ful years in Brooklyn, my dad bought another candy store in Woodhaven, Queens. It was a true fixer-upper. The store was dark and dingy with peeling paint, creaking floors, grimy, nic-otine-stained woodwork, and glass that hadn't been cleaned in decades.

Dad hired a contractor to remodel the store, which caused a lot of speculation, gossip, and envy among the other candy store owners.

There were five candy stores within a two-block radius, each vying for its own turf. At that time, candy stores sold newspapers, cigars, cigarettes, ice cream, and candy, along with gifts and greeting cards, but it was cigarette prices that the stores battled over. Each store owner undercut the price of cigarettes in an attempt to attract customers, thereby losing money in the process.

My dad thought this was senseless and caused a lot of unnec-essary stress. He wanted to convince the store owners to keep cigarette prices stable. When the wholesaler raised the prices, they would raise the selling price by the same amount. Customers would patronize the store that they preferred instead of jumping around trying to save a penny.

Dad loved people and took a special interest in each and every customer. He treated the customers like family. He loved telling stories and hated losing a customer over a penny for a pack of cigarettes.

The day arrived when his proposal to stabilize cigarette prices among the five stores was to be presented to Old Man Levy and his wife across the street. I was 12 years old and I can still remember the eerie scene as we entered their dark and dreary store with floorboards so worn you could see streams of light coming up from the basement.

With the other four store owners present, my dad began by saying, "Cutting prices on each other and losing money doesn't make much sense." He continued with his case for ending the cigarette war.

After hearing him out, Old Lady Levy said in a heavy Eastern European accent, "Itz okay by me, but vat about dat son of a bitsh across da street?"

Without missing a beat, my father stepped forward and said, "I'm that son of a bitch across the street."

After a few moments of utter silence, when it felt like the air was being sucked out of the room, my father started to laugh. The other store owners gulped and nervously started laughing. The agreement was finally reached, and from that time on a much more peaceful competition ensued.

Dad in front of his Woodhaven, Queens, candy store

Losing Patience with Hilda

Most of the customers at my dad's candy store were friendly and courteous. They all loved my dad. Except for Hilda. This older German lady was a real pain in the butt and tried my dad's patience on many occasions. She was abrasive, demanding, and always in a rush. You could feel the energy shift as she walked through the door, instantly putting everyone on edge.

The busiest time of day at the store was between 5:30 and 6:30 p.m. Folks were getting home from work and stopping at the store for a pack of cigarettes, a cigar, or a box of candy for the wife.

One day at rush hour, my dad was behind the counter, I was assisting a customer, and my mother was drinking a cup of coffee. Hilda was about 35 feet away in the new greeting card section. When Dad had remodeled the store, he had streamlined its operation by creating self-service card racks with storage drawers below.

All of a sudden, Hilda let out a shriek from across the crowded store. "Mr. Vite, Mr. Vite, vere should I poot dis extra envelope?" she cried out from the greeting card section.

My father was completely taken by surprise and, in a knee-jerk reaction, shouted back in Yiddish, "Schtek es en tuchas!" ("Stick it up your ass!")

I dropped what I was doing and howled with laughter. My mother spit out a mouthful of coffee, creating a gusher that landed all over the boxes of Whitman's Samplers that I had just carefully arranged. Luckily, they were protected by cellophane.

Happily, we never saw Hilda again.

Annie and Whitey's Fiftieth

"**L**a Petite Marmite in Palm Beach is Mom and Dad's favorite."
"Oh Kenny, that's much too fancy," my sister protested.
"But they eat there all the time," I said.

I was living in Los Angeles, Marlene lived in New Jersey, and Mom and Dad lived in Florida. Logistically, pulling together an anniversary party for them in Florida was difficult but not impossible.

To make my sister more comfortable, I sent her a menu from the restaurant with a few entrée suggestions. After some cajoling, she reluctantly agreed, and we began compiling a guest list of family and friends.

"Do you have any thoughts about the invitations?" I asked.

"Invitations? Why do we need invitations? My friend Norma just threw a 50th birthday party for her husband. She just called up everyone, we went to their house, she served sloppy joes, and we all had a swell time."

Right then I knew we were in trouble and this was going to be an uphill battle. I finally convinced her to go along with invitations that I would design, print, and pay for. However, I still needed the guest list. This was before the internet, so after many phone calls and letters, we had a guest list of 50 people.

"Since we have so many guests, the manager will give us an area in the dining room near the patio," I explained to Marlene on one of our many planning calls. "I was also thinking it would be lovely if we had a violinist playing classical and Yiddish music while we're having dinner."

"What, me pay for music to entertain the whole restaurant?" she shouted over the phone.

That's when I absolutely knew this could escalate into *The War of the Roses*, and we hadn't even decided on the menu or the budget. My blood pressure was rising, the joy and the fun of planning the party was gone, and I was close to calling the whole thing off.

After I cooled down a bit, I called my sister and said, "Marlene, I love you, honey, but this is no longer fun for me. I don't work well with committees and never have. Let's just establish a budget, and either you do the party completely and I will give you a check for half, or I'll do the party and you pay me for half. I throw lots of parties and I know how to make it fun, beautiful, and memorable. Just let me know what you decide."

"Okay, Kenny, I'll discuss it with Ted and get back to you."

The next day she called me and, to my amazement, said, "Ted and I agreed to let you do the party."

I was thrilled, even though the full responsibility was now on me.

We amicably decided on the menu and the budget. I found some great boxes of stationery with a lovely floral border at a store in Beverly Hills. The salesman recommended a calligrapher who would hand letter the invitations and address the envelopes for us. They turned out to be beautiful and elegant and set the tone for the whole event. Now I was having fun!

The maître d' at La Petite Marmite sent me business cards of several violinists and an accordion player. I chose the violinist with the most professional business card, praying I chose well.

I flew to Palm Beach a few days before the event to meet with the owner of the restaurant, the florist, and a party rental company to choose tablecloths, napkins, and stemware. My sister would have had a fit if she were present. Paper and plastic would have been her choices.

The day of the party was approaching, and friends and relatives were arriving by plane, bus, train, and automobile. I was excited and a bit nervous. I loved family gatherings, but pulling something like this off long distance was not in my playbook.

I arrived at La Petite Marmite an hour early to make sure everything was in place. To my surprise, the manager of the restaurant gave us a private room that was previously unavailable. I was thrilled.

However, the table linens I ordered did not arrive. The restaurant had some special mauve table linens that actually complemented the centerpieces' bright pink rubrum lilies, white tulips, and lily of the valley. Another happy accident.

A rather short gentleman in a tuxedo arrived carrying an accordion case. My heart sank as he said, "Are you Mr. White?"

"Yes, who are you?"

"I'm Morey. You hired me for your folks' anniversary party."

"What? I thought you were a violinist."

I thumbed through the folder with all my notes and realized I had called the wrong number. I called the accordionist, not the violinist. Oye!

"Now, Mr. White, don't you worry, I've got this covered," Morey assured me. "We are going to have a great party. I guarantee it."

I was speechless. What to do? Either go with Morey or create a scene and have no music at all. After swallowing hard and taking a few deep breaths, I said, "Morey, you're our man."

We shook hands and discussed the type of music I preferred, and I let Morey take it from there. And take over he did. He was not just a musician—he was an incredible master of ceremonies and a wedding singer. He played all the music you'd expect at a Jewish wedding, including Klezmer, the music of the Ashkenazi Jews and our family.

My heart was bursting with joy as our friends and family arrived to Morey's soulful accordion music. My mom and dad came in last as Morey played Wagner's "Bridal Chorus"—also known as "Here Comes the Bride." There was not a dry eye in the place. My mom was delighted but embarrassed by all the attention. Dad ate it up. His hands flew up in the air as he snapped his fingers to the beat of the Klezmer music. I was in heaven and realized we hit a home run. This was the last joyful event where our whole family was happy, alive, and together.

The Gift

After two emergency surgeries, Dad started exploring alternative healing, health foods, vitamins, and food supplements. This was radical thinking in the 1950s.

Dr. Schields, one of Dad's favorite customers, was a chiropractor and became our go-to doctor. Chiropractic treatment was an emerging phenomenon at the time. My mother initially pooh-poohed it but later accepted and embraced it. Dad also investigated yoga, Buddhism, Hinduism, and other spiritual and alternative thought processes. However, he was not a purist, and he enjoyed smoking cigars and delighted in eating a fresh ham sandwich every once in a while.

Rudy's German Deli was the pride of the neighborhood and right next door to Dad's candy store. I can still taste the tangy German potato salad made with vinegar and the delicious ham my father introduced me to when I was 12.

Even though my dad was a health food nut, he ate almost anything, and ham was his favorite. My mother, on the other hand, kept a strictly kosher home. She was not into health food and never ate pork or shellfish—even in a Chinese restaurant.

When my mother wasn't in earshot, Dad would ask me to go next door and have Rudy make him a ham sandwich with lots of dark mustard on pumpernickel bread. In case my mother overheard us, we used our code name for ham: roast beef. The ham tasted even better knowing it was forbidden.

This small secret that we shared was big for me and created a special bond between the two of us. I can't eat a ham or a roast beef sandwich without thinking of my dad and our clandestine moments together.

At 86, Dad flew to Los Angeles to be part of my 50th birthday celebration. Mom had died the previous fall. My good friend Harvey arranged a roast, à la Dean Martin, complete with a podium, amplification system, and theatrical lighting with double pink gels to make everyone look young and vibrant, especially me. I thought I was old at 50.

In addition to all the love and laughter that was showered on me from my friends and family, Dad created the tearjerker of the evening. He took the stage, told a few jokes in the style of George Burns, and gave a heartfelt and touching speech praising me.

"Ya know, this guy here that you are honoring tonight, he had bigger balls than his old man," Dad said. "He put himself through school and left New York, his rent-controlled apartment, and everything familiar. He worked, studied, bought real estate, and started his own successful business. He took lots of chances and created an incredible life full of friends and people who adore him. As a father, I couldn't be prouder."

After he spoke, there was not a dry eye in the room. By the time the evening was over, everyone had fallen in love with him.

Dad was the gift

What we lacked in closeness and intimacy in our early years was paid for in full on that June evening in Los Angeles.

I had said some hurtful things to him that I regret to this day, like after my 50th birthday party when we were sitting in my living room opening up my gifts. There was none from him. *My dad didn't buy me a birthday present.* I was deeply hurt, which brought up all my disappointments as a child, and I told him so. I reverted back to being a hurt little boy even though I was 50 years old.

Now looking back with more mature eyes, I can see that *he* was the gift. By flying three thousand miles to my landmark birthday celebration and praising me to the sky to all my friends and colleagues, there couldn't have been a greater gift.

Dad with my cousin, Norman, laughing at my
50th birthday party

My Other Two Sisters

The call came from Dr. Cohen, my father's longtime cardiologist. He informed me that my dad was in critical condition at a hospital in Palm Beach.

"Ken, didn't you know that your dad is in the ICU?" asked Dr. Cohen.

I was in shock but stuttered, "N—no, no, I didn't. I'll take the next flight out."

My folks had lived in Florida for 25 years and had been in moderately good health for most of it. My mother, however, had died six years prior. Whitey had a warm smile, a ready joke, and a compassionate ear. He was adored by almost everyone who knew him.

When I arrived at the hospital, I saw him hooked up to every machine known to modern science. He had yards of tubing coming and going into every orifice. IV drips were continually feeding him food and medication. These were the *heroic measures* that he had signed documents to avoid. It was a horror show that no one at 91 deserves.

Dad made it through the three weeks of medical procedures and was as weak as a kitten. He now needed bed rest and 24-hour care. Though frail, he was in full charge of his faculties. He and I discussed the options of getting round-the-clock care at home or going to a skilled nursing facility. Home care, which would be expensive and difficult for me to manage long distance, would come out of his pocket. Without much trepidation he said, "Fuck 'em, let the insurance companies pay for it." So we opted for a nursing facility.

We were hoping for a brief stay so he could then continue living independently. Up to this point, Dad had been extremely active and was still president of his condo association.

I called Dr. Cohen and asked if he made house calls to nursing homes. He replied, "You're not going to send Whitey to a nursing home, are you?"

I was devastated by his remark. I was already suffering from tremendous guilt and remorse of even thinking of putting my dad in a nursing home. This conversation just added to my distress.

I informed him that I needed to return to Santa Fe. The doctor obviously cared about my dad. He asked, "What about your sisters?"

I explained that my sister lived in New Jersey, had MS, and needed day-to-day care herself.

"What about your other sisters?" Dr. Cohen asked.

"What other sisters?" I asked.

"The nuns."

I broke out laughing and realized the comedy that was now unfolding. It seemed that the doctor was another victim of my dad's sense of humor.

The nuns joke originated from one of the customers of my dad's candy store in Woodhaven. Kathleen had been buying gum, penny candy, and greeting cards for several years and had become a cherished customer. After high school she left to attend a seminary for girls. Several years later, she sent Dad a picture of herself and a friend in their nuns' habits posing on the grounds in front of their convent. He carried that picture in his wallet for over 40 years, jokingly telling everyone that these were his two daughters.

Obviously, Dr. Cohen didn't know my father was Jewish and that he had been taken in by this incredible yarn, as had countless others. I explained the background and circumstances of the picture to the doctor, and we both had a good chuckle.

After a long and arduous search, I finally found a beautiful, upscale skilled nursing facility that was immediately available.

We transferred my dad on Wednesday afternoon, and I kissed him goodbye and left for Santa Fe the following Friday. My dad died 24 hours later as he laughed his way into the next world.

Sister Kathleen (left) and a friend

Whitey's Funeral

Teddy, my brother-in-law, handled all the arrangements with Knollwood Park Cemetery and the funeral in Brooklyn.

I called my old friend Joel to tell him about Whitey's passing and invite him to come to the funeral. At that time, he was the vice president of pastoral care for a New York hospital on Long Island.

"Kenny, of course I'll be there," Father Joel said in the gentlest, most comforting tone. "Do you want me to come in full drag with the white collar or just a black suit and a cross?"

Joel Harvey, formerly Joel Smolensky, a Jewish Brooklyn boy, was now an Episcopalian priest and one of the funniest men on the planet. He was also once a child actor and appeared in the original *The King and I* on Broadway. Jokingly he said, "At eight, I was already a has-been."

"The black suit and white collar will be perfect."

"The big silver cross or the smaller one?"

"Oh, Joel, wear the big silver one with Jesus on it. Whitey would love it."

My dad was totally irreverent when it came to religious rituals.

* * *

When I arrived at the funeral, Teddy handed me a tie. In the Jewish tradition, the tie or a piece of cloth of the mourner is torn at the funeral as an expression of grief or loss.

"Kenny, here's an old tie from work," Teddy said. "I know you usually wear expensive ones. So why ruin yours."

25

I put my designer tie in my pocket and put on Teddy's. The rabbi took out his knife and began cutting the men's ties. He got to my tie and began cutting, but the fabric would not tear. He sawed and sawed at it, but it wouldn't give.

It was made from some indestructible fiber. I think they wrap spaceships in it to protect the ship from the heat of reentry. The rabbi began to sweat, and the mourners smiled and then laughed. I'm sure my father got a chuckle out of it too because as they lowered the coffin, the lid clipped the side of the grave, popped open, and then slammed shut. I think it was Whitey's way of saying goodbye. A jokester till the end.

Whitey (Dad) at 86 in Santa Barbara, California

Stewart, My Friend, My Mentor

We met at Brooklyn Tech, an all-boys high school for serious and gifted students who were planning on going into architecture or one of the engineering fields.

Our local high school was rumored to be a hotbed of marijuana and other drugs that nice Jewish boys shouldn't be involved in. At 12 I was angry, confused, lacked self-confidence, and was overwhelmed by life and my parents' attitudes and opinions. If it weren't for low self-esteem, I wouldn't have had any. It was my mother's idea for me to study and take the entrance exam for Brooklyn Tech. My hormones were raging, as was the drive to grow up and get the hell out of her house. My father was just another passenger on this ship of discontent.

Stewart was a gawky, nerdy kid who sidled up next to me in chemistry class. We began hanging out in the cafeteria and sometimes after school.

We discovered our mutual secret in the bathroom at Howard Johnson across from Radio City Music Hall. Stewart and I checked each other out at the urinals for much longer than most straight guys did. We discovered that we were kindred spirits and became close friends.

In the late '50s and early '60s, the term gay was not widely used. Before that, you were either queer, homosexual, or a fag.

Stewart was living in Brooklyn with his divorced mother and elderly grandmother. I was living with my mother and father in a one-bedroom apartment in Queens. My sister and I shared a bedroom till she was 21 and I was 17. When she married and moved out, my parents took the bedroom, and I slept on a sofa bed in the living room. Stu and I were both unhappy, frustrated, and hiding our enormous secret. Freida, Stewart's mother, was a psychic vampire who whined with the shrill of a cat in heat. My mother, Annie, was a rage-o-holic who thrived on discontent, tempered by Valium and phenobarbital.

We both graduated Brooklyn Tech in 1958. I got a job with a decorating firm, making minimum wage. Stewart worked part time for his uncle Alex who owned and operated Sunnydale Farms, a successful dairy in Brooklyn.

"Stewart, I've got to get out of this crazy house," I'd say. "I can't take it anymore. Let's get an apartment together."

Several months later he called me. "Kenny, I found a one-bedroom, rent-controlled apartment in Brooklyn Heights. It's fifty-six dollars and eighteen cents a month. It's filthy dirty and needs a lot of work."

"Take it," I screamed. "I don't care what it looks like. We'll clean it up. Give them a deposit."

One week later I met Stewart in front of 136 Montague Street, a vintage brownstone that would be my home for the next five years. The agent took us up the timeworn wooden steps to apartment number three. My heart was beating out of my chest. I was so excited to finally sense the possibility of freedom and a new home.

The agent opened the door, and all I could see were generations of filth and squalor. An old gas stove sat in the middle of the living room along with an ancient refrigerator with a round, pineapple-shaped motor sitting on top. It had a closed-off fireplace, tall bay windows, and old, grimy, stained hardwood floors that needed refinishing. Several species of cockroaches, both living and dead, covered the floors. To me it was a palace in the making. Finally! A place of our own.

We signed the lease, received the keys, and began our plan. The landlord was going to provide a new refrigerator and stove, but the painting and restoration was up to us. He did provide the paint, however. Stewart and I both went to Pratt Institute at night and worked during the day. How we got it all done is still a mystery to me, but we did.

Move-in day was approaching, and my parents didn't know that I was moving out. It was a subject that was off limits. Actually, most subjects were off limits if it didn't conform to my mother's fear-driven way of thinking.

The plan was set in motion. Sid, Stewart's brother-in-law, rented a U-Haul trailer and hooked it up to his car. We waited until my mother and father were out of the house, picked up my desk, my clothes, and all my school stuff, and stole into the night. Stewart's move was less dramatic. He just told his mother he was leaving. His grandmother said to him, "So Stewart, ya goin' to live mit da ha-mach-shu-als (homosexuals)?" That was the laugh that sustained us throughout the move.

I was less courageous and left my parents a note. The shit hit the fan the very next day when I called them.

"What do you mean you're moving out?" my mother said. "What am I going to tell the family?"

This infuriated me. It made me realize that my mother was more concerned with what people thought than how I felt.

"Ma, I moved out, I'm not *moving* out. Stewart and I took an apartment together in Brooklyn Heights."

"And the desk, you took the desk?"

"You gave me the desk as a present."

"Yes, but it wasn't yours to take."

The anger, the hurt, and the pleading went on for half an hour before I finally hung up.

I called my sister later that day.

"Marlene, I moved out of the house and took an apartment with Stewart."

"Kenny, that's terrific. The only mistake you made is that you should have done it years ago."

Those were the most reassuring and affirming words that could have been spoken. I was guilt-ridden, insecure, and had no self-confidence. I needed to be told by someone I trusted that I did the right thing.

Working on the apartment was arduous but joyful. The building was designed and built as a mansion in 1883. At the beginning of the Depression, it was subdivided into stores on the street level and apartments above. We had the choice location facing Montague Street. It had 12-foot ceilings, bay windows, in-laid hardwood floors, and a painted-over white marble fireplace.

Seventy-five years of paint and wallpaper had to be removed to reveal the smooth plaster walls and deep crown moldings. In the bathroom, black vinyl wallpaper with pink and turquoise flamingos hid a deep crack in the walls that was home to a nest of cockroaches. The slow transformation gave me a sense of pride and belonging. It became home.

Stewart, whose family didn't have a dime, was raised with his wealthy cousins. They introduced him to Broadway, the theater, ballet, movies, and the joy of laughter. He had also been shown the opera, museums, and literature by his older gay male friends. This was the legacy he passed on to me.

"Kenny, meet me at the Four Seasons for a drink after work," he'd say. I didn't know this world existed. Nor did I know how to set a proper table or which fork or wine glass to use. I only knew what I learned in school, at work, or at my dad's candy store. Stewart was my mentor.

While I stayed home, scraping and painting, Stewart was out hitting the clubs. Even though we were not lovers, I assumed we had an equal partnership in the apartment. It was never clearly expressed or understood. I was angry and deeply resentful. I did all the work while he was out partying. This created a huge rift in our relationship.

Then there was the shower curtain incident—the straw that broke the camel's back. Our tiny bathroom had a claw-foot porcelain tub with a circular rod that held a grimy old plastic shower curtain. Once the walls were painted, we needed a new curtain. We could barely pay the rent and tuition, eat, and go to a movie once a month. So I said, "Let's just buy a cheap, clear plastic liner for now."

The next day Stewart came home with a beige moiré satin shower curtain from Abraham & Strauss.

It cost $20.

I was livid because we couldn't afford it. I resented paying for half, and I hated the boring beige color. Twenty dollars back then is what $200 is today. We barely spoke again for about six months, even though we lived together. Our different work and school schedules made it easy for us to avoid one another. Eventually, I picked up some freelance design work and could afford the place by myself. Stewart left the apartment and moved to California to reconnect with his estranged father and siblings.

Five years later, I moved to Los Angeles and decided to look him up. The shower curtain incident was now just a memory. I longed for the close friendship we once had. I called him, and we met for lunch. After catching up with our lives and telling stories about our old friends and families, the five years we lost just melted away. We were back to becoming good buddies again. He was no longer my mentor; I now knew which fork to use.

Several years later, the roles reversed. I started an interior design firm, employed several people, owned my own home, and had income property and a savings account. Stewart worked for several architectural firms, rented an apartment, and spent much more than he made. To say he didn't know how to manage money was a gross understatement. There were periods of unemployment that were a tremendous struggle for him.

Who knew that I would become the stable one?

Through some stroke of luck, Sylvester Stallone hired Stewart to design his new home in Bel Air, a very posh area above Beverly Hills. The project was enormous, and Stewart was very capable and had great communication skills. It was quite a plum that would have a net profit of over $100,000. Stu did a beautiful job, and Stallone was pleased.

With several bankruptcies and numerous creditors calling daily, the idea of Stewart having a legitimate bank account was out of the question. Banks had to report income to creditors when names were flagged, and he had no intention of paying off his debts.

"What should I do? They're paying me in cash," he asked me.

"Take the hundred-dollar bills and staple them together in packs of ten, then put the stacks in a safety deposit box. Don't touch it for six months until you come up with a plan."

That was like asking an alcoholic on a bender not to take a drink. Stewart and Mason, a younger boyfriend from Beverly Hills, got high one afternoon and went shopping. The next day, I got the call.

"Kenny, let's get together for dinner," Stewart said. "I've got some new things I want to show you."

I went to his apartment and was genuinely impressed with the cashmere Canali suits, vicuna sports jackets, Gucci shoes and ties, all laid out on the bed.

"Holy shit, Stewart, what did you do?"

"Mason and I went shopping. Whattaya think?"

Not wanting to be a downer and a scolding parent, I said, "Wow, Stu, these threads are incredible. I'd hate to ask how much they cost."

I admired everything and tried to share in his joy and the momentary high. Needless to say, the $100,000 didn't last very long. Limousines, five-star restaurants, and high living were his cocaine, in addition to the stuff he blew up his nose.

In happy times, we would celebrate our birthdays together since we were born 11 days apart. To commemorate the occasion, we would choose a new or trendy hotel and check in for the weekend.

The New Otani Hotel had recently opened in Little Tokyo, near downtown Los Angeles. It had a Kyoto-style rooftop garden with classic Japanese water features and streams. The hotel was offering a promotional rate for our auspicious birthday weekend. It included an overnight stay in an authentic Japanese suite, dinner for two, a shiatsu massage, and a complimentary bottle of sake.

We checked into the Osaka suite, complete with shoji screens and a raised floor with tatami mats customized to fit the room. Folded neatly near the entrance were two indigo-blue kimonos on a golden teak bench. A traditional Japanese tea ceremony, including the cups, pot, and all the implements, was already set up for us.

Stewart and I looked at each other in disbelief as we were taken in by this exotic sight. We had hit the jackpot!

There was a soft knock on the door as we were informed about our massage appointments and were respectfully escorted across the rooftop garden to the spa area. I was hoping for a hot Japanese male masseur but was met by Koharu, who looked like a female sumo wrestler. I was definitely in for a no-nonsense, intense massage. Six massage tables were lined up and separated by a thin white cotton curtain. There was no real privacy. Everything could be heard if not seen. No hanky-panky here.

After our massages, we showered and relaxed before dinner. What came next was completely unexpected. Our bathroom had a built-in, cobalt-blue–tiled step-in soaking tub. We decided to have a soak before dinner when Stu lit up a joint and handed it to me. I rarely smoked pot, but this was a special occasion, so I accepted.

Our 40-year friendship morphed into a safe, but frisky, carnal evening. I was shocked and promised myself to never to tell a living soul. So much for promises.

* * *

Tom Rolla, a friend of Stewart, was starting a supper club on Melrose Avenue in West Hollywood and hired Stewart to design it. Stewart's design for The Gardenia Room was simplified elegance and very chic. He used soft peach walls with a series of circular mirrors surrounding the main room. A cleverly placed pin-spot lighted a single flower on each linen-draped table. The main lighting was focused on the ebony baby grand piano where legendary entertainers would perform. Melba Moore, who was one of Stewart's favorites, performed the night of the opening. The Gardenia became a huge success and is now celebrating its 39th year.

* * *

Stewart was talented, kind, and generous to a fault. He knew the best and aspired to the best.

"You don't have to stay at the Four Seasons, but you can certainly afford to go there for a drink," he'd say.

When Stewart had money in his pocket, nothing was too good, and he invited you along for the ride, but when he was broke, keep your hands on your wallet. On many occasions, he would call up a group of friends, arrange a dinner at Le Dome, Scandia, or the trendiest restaurant in town. The food was usually fabulous, because he knew great food. Champagne and expensive drinks would flow, and Stewart would inaudibly direct the waiter to give *you* the check. Oftentimes, during his broke period, he even showed up in a limousine. Credit cards were his nemesis. We all knew this and still loved him.

Ken and Stewart in Las Vegas in 1986

Throwing Mort Out

It was a perfect spring day in New York City. The air was fresh and crisp, and the profuse beds of yellow and white daffodils along Park Avenue were ablaze with color.

Walking south on my way back from lunch, I was stopped in my tracks by this striking vision: a drop-dead gorgeous six-foot-two hunk of a man. He passed me and turned around, and I did the same. We exchanged evocative glances; he approached me, and we traded phone numbers with the promise of getting together.

He said he was unhappily married with two children. I was so taken by him and his good looks that I seemed to gloss over the fact that I would be "the other woman," even though we had barely met.

We had lunch the next day and dinner the next night in my Brooklyn Heights apartment.

All the red warning lights were diverted by passion or ignored entirely. I had just celebrated my 20th birthday; I worked as an entry-level design assistant and went to Pratt Institute at night. Mort, at 35, was a creative director for a major advertising agency. As time went on, he helped me with my homework, and I helped him with more salacious endeavors.

Shortly thereafter, his wife threw him out and divorced him. Stewart, my roommate, was moving to California, so Mort moved in. We lasted less than a year when I discovered him screwing all my friends, even the ones that were committed to celibacy. That's when I learned about the term sociopath. I threw him out.

* * *

After arriving in West Hollywood in 1964, I had rekindled my friendship with Stewart. We met for lunch at Ed's coffee shop, the unofficial hub of the interior design business. Stewart had a job with a commercial firm that designed and furnished offices and business interiors.

We chatted and laughed about our separation as we had lunch.

"I'm working on the new Max Factor building on Hollywood Boulevard, and you'll never guess who I ran into."

I couldn't even imagine whom he was referring to.

"Mort," he said.

My jaw dropped. I was speechless.

"He moved out here and started dating Barbara Factor."

"Max Factor's daughter?" I asked in amazement.

"Yes, after a short courtship, they were married, and he became vice president in charge of advertising."

Nothing like screwing your way to the top, I thought.

"The wildest part is when I went to meet with the Max Factor executives," Stewart said excitedly. "I interviewed each one individually to discuss the type of desks and furniture they preferred. I was led to Mort's office in their old building on Highland Avenue. He greeted me, shook my hand, locked the door, and pulled my zipper down. It was like watching a porno movie, except I was one of the principal players."

"Holy shit, Stewart, that sounds just like Mort. How long did the project take?"

"Six months. I was drained by the time they moved into the new building on Hollywood Boulevard."

"Stu, I think you should sell the movie rights to this story, but you'll have to wait till everyone's dead to get it produced."

Sometime later, Stewart and I were having lunch at Ed's coffee shop when in walked Mort. Barbara Factor had recently divorced him and threw him out. He was living on his boat in Marina del Rey.

He acted as if no time had passed and that I didn't know he'd just had sex with Stewart. He invited us both back to his boat for a three-way. That's when it all came back to me and I was reminded of the time when I was 20 and *I threw him out.*

Stewart in Paris

Stewart was living in Paris with Yves Vidal, the president of Knoll International. Well, that's what he led me to believe. Actually, he was just seeing Yves. The truth and the details are buried somewhere on the Left Bank or in a fine bottle of Beaujolais.

Just knowing that Stewart was in Paris gave me the courage and confidence to plan my first trip abroad. It was 1968, and I had just turned 28.

When planning my trip, Stewart said, "Kenny, you have to take the TEE (Trans-Europe Express) train from Amsterdam to Paris and have lunch in its first-class dining car. It's an experience you won't forget."

I booked my first-class seat and dining reservation exactly as directed. The dining car was mostly occupied by well-dressed European tourists. The fine linens, silverware, and glassware rivaled any five-star restaurant in the States. The waiter, dressed in a tuxedo, showed me to my table and delivered a menu. Speaking through his nose, he said something to me in indistinguishable French. The luncheon menu was two feet tall and cumbersome. Always uncomfortable eating alone in a formal restaurant, I nervously perused the menu, not recognizing a single item. I had eaten in many French restaurants in New York City and studied French in high school, but still I was stymied.

I signaled for the waiter and asked, "Monsieur, s'il vous plaît, aidez-moi a commander." Which I thought meant, "Please help me order."

All I got back from him was *fah, fah, fah,* as he took my order with an upturned nose. I had heard that the French were arrogant, but I hadn't experienced it until that moment.

As I sipped a glass of expensive chardonnay, my order arrived. First, what I thought was a salad was potatoes au gratin on greens I didn't recognize. Then came another unrecognizable dish of another kind of potato. All in all, there were five potato dishes that this asshole waiter helped me order. I was incensed, but he only spoke French and would say, "Je ne comprends pas."

I was fuming as I reluctantly put the charge on my credit card and left no tip. *That* gesture, in any language, is still the same.

Stewart was waiting for me at Gare du Nord, the busiest train station in Europe. He was a welcome sight indeed. He was much thinner than I had remembered from six months earlier but seemed happy as we chatted on and on. I couldn't wait to tell him the story of my very first French encounter. It had to be all uphill from there.

After hailing a taxi, we made our way to the Hotel Crystal on the Left Bank. From the meager price of the room, I knew we were not staying at the Ritz, but it was far below my expectations. We had discussed it earlier and had decided to spend our money on food and entertainment instead. I soon found out that it wasn't *our* money but *my* money we were spending. Stewart was down to his last $5, and I wound up supporting him for the next two weeks.

Our shabby room had tall ceilings and dirty windows that faced a brick wall. A clothesline held two printed cotton sheets, separating the room for privacy. It would be used only when either Stewart or I entertained gentlemen callers.

In contrast to the accommodations was our lunch the following day with Yves Vidal. We met at the newly remodeled Knoll showroom and walked to an intimate French restaurant. Yves was a good-looking, charming middle-aged man, obviously quite taken with Stewart. I was a bit envious but made every attempt to be gracious. I was able to pay for my own lunch, but Yves insisted on picking up the check. Before leaving the restaurant, he showed us the latest Knoll catalogue, featuring photographs of an ancient water-driven grain mill right in the heart of Paris. It was actually his home and the backdrop for the new Knoll furniture catalogue. The chic modern furniture was set against medieval tapestries hanging on rustic stone walls. It was breathtaking! The rest of the catalogue showed more of his home and the rest of the line of furniture.

Lunch ended with shaking hands and kissing the air above each cheek. Stewart and I spent the rest of the day visiting Notre-Dame and walking along the Seine. It was a perfect way to bask in the glow of our visit to Notre-Dame and having lunch with Yves Vidal.

The next night, we were on our own and ate at one of the landmark restaurants on the Left Bank. Roger la Grenouille was started in the 1930s and became a favorite hangout for the Allied fighter pilots during World War II. Roger Spinhirny, the owner, took care of and fed the deprived and downtrodden during the war. Every Thursday he offered free food to the orphans of Paris. Pictures and memorabilia of the restaurant's history lined the weathered walls. The simple, tasty, and affordable food drew us there night after night.

Sitting at group tables, we mixed and mingled with the locals and tourists from all over Europe. The energy reached a crescendo one night when the waitstaff brought out the ice cream and banana dessert and removed all the utensils. The banana was sticking straight up between two balls of chocolate ice cream. "How do you eat this thing?" we asked. That's when the fun began.

* * *

One night, Stewart had a date, so I decided to go to one of the local bars. He gave me directions to Le Drugstore, a high-end department store featuring perfumes, gift items, drugs, and a see-and-be-seen lunch counter. Behind Le Drugstore was a dimly lit alley right out of a scene from Brecht's *Threepenny Opera*. I looked for nombre seven as instructed and went up to the blackened door and knocked three times. When the small peephole opened, I uttered the code, "Je suis comme ça" ("I am like that"). It gave me entry into a slightly scary but intriguing world of fun and adventure. The walls were painted black, and the only visible lighting was over the pool table and the illuminated signs advertising beer or wine. I watched the guys playing pool and tried to make contact, but my flirting and language skills didn't take me very far. I left and went around the corner to Le Drugstore, had a brioche, and went back to the hotel, assuming Stewart had already concluded his evening. He hadn't, so I made my apologies, pulled the curtain, and went to sleep.

The next morning, Stewart, Jean Pierre (the gentleman of the evening), and I got up and went around the corner to Café de Flore for coffee and a croissant. Jean Pierre turned out to be a delightful young man. We all got along famously and spent the rest of the day and evening together. This time we didn't need to pull the curtain.

Jean Pierre hung out with us for the next two days. He recommended Le Soufflé, a restaurant located on a narrow street near the Louvre. It was also featured in the current Michelin guide to Paris.

The walls and windows of Le Soufflé were draped in a creamy-beige fabric. Paintings hung on wires in front of the draped walls as crystal chandeliers sparkled and illuminated the room. We were escorted down a hallway to a smaller room that held four round tables. It was a perfect spot for a clandestine affair. As the name implied, the restaurant specialized in soufflés of every type imaginable. We ordered a citrus salad and a chicken soufflé. The butter lettuce salad had a delicate dressing garnished with slices of blood orange and raspberries. A six-inch-high soufflé arrived on a silver tray. The waiter took the cover off of a clay crock, revealing an extraordinary chicken, mushroom, and carrot ragout. He then ladled the savory stew, piercing the center of the soufflé. I gasped. It looked like he was ruining this gorgeous soufflé. But he didn't ruin it at all. In fact, the blended ingredients enhanced the soufflé as it absorbed all its juices and flavors. I was in culinary heaven. For dessert, I had the raspberry, and Stewart had the chocolate soufflé. It was served in the same way with the sauce spooned into the center of a smaller soufflé ramekin. God, was that good!

As my vacation came to an end, I bid Stewart goodbye. He was moving in with Allan Lazar, a longtime friend. Stewart had no money, and my wallet had shrunk considerably, but I gave him a hundred-dollar bill, wished him well, and took a taxi to the airport.

After I left Paris, Yves invited Stewart to the grand opening for his new furniture collection. Not having any money and wanting to dress to impress, Stewart flew to London on his soon-to-expire American Airlines credit card, went to Harrods on another credit card, and bought a suit, sports jacket, three shirts, shoes, socks, and ties. He had the suit tailored on a rush order, as he was having lunch in Harrods' first-class dining room. Before flying back to Paris, he had high tea at Fortnum & Mason with no intention to pay for any of it before filing for bankruptcy. This happened minutes before they shut down all his credit cards. I was aghast as he openly boasted to me of what he had just done.

All his other friends who truly loved this crazy, zany guy, would throw up their hands and say, "Oh well, that's Stewart."

Blessed in Chimayo

El Santuario de Chimayo in northern New Mexico is a 17th-century Roman Catholic shrine and pilgrimage site. Besides the miracles and the myths, the church has a rustic splendor that, to my mind, is unparalleled in the United States. "This dirt floor is considered 'holy soil' with extraordinary healing powers," the young priest at the church would say to visitors.

In the summer of 1993, Stewart visited me at my new home in Santa Fe. As an unofficial tour guide of the Southwest, I put the town of Chimayo and its church on the top of our list.

As Stewart and I entered the legendary shrine, we were struck by the enormous hand-hewn beams and the three-foot-thick adobe walls that supported the massive structure. Primitively carved statues and the vibrant tempera-colored altar were radiantly lit by hundreds of burning devotional candles.

Father Joseph approached us. "Where are you guys from? What brings you to Chimayo?" It was the usual chatty conversation that takes place in any tourist town or gay bar, we thought.

"I'm from San Francisco," Stewart replied.

"I live in Santa Fe," I added.

We carried on the conversation with the priest, who graciously asked, "Would you like me to give you a blessing?"

Stewart and I looked at each other and thought, *Why not? It's free! What can it hurt? We're Jewish, but we're not Orthodox.*

We followed the priest into a side office that was a modern addition to the church, where the conversation continued. The priest took out a bowl of holy water, said some prayers, and blessed us both with a light sprinkling. We placed a donation into the offering box and left with burning questions.

"Was he coming on to us and we didn't pick up on it? If he was more attractive, would we have pursued it?" Stewart asked.

"Yes, yes, and definitely yes." We both agreed.

Six months passed, and I got a call from Stewart, who was still living in San Francisco.

"Remember the church in Chimayo?"

"Yes, of course I do."

"I was telling our story of the young priest to Maxine. Remember my sister Maxine who converted from Judaism and became a Catholic nun?"

"Yes, how could I forget Maxine with the big tits?"

"Well, she said we were not only blessed, but we also were baptized."

We both howled till our sides hurt.

Whether it was true or not is still a mystery. It remains one of my fondest and funniest memories of my dear friend Stewart.

Real Wall-to-Wall Carpet

Looking down at the rose-colored carpet and knowing it was actually linoleum was a huge turnoff. Even as a kid, I knew without a doubt, there had to be a more luxurious way to live. I prayed that one day we'd move out of my grandmother's house and I'd finally get my own room and make my own decorating choices.

In 1952, I got my wish. My dad bought an old-fashioned candy store, and we moved out of my grandmother's house into a rented apartment close to the new store. I worked there every day after school. My job was to stack crates of bottled sodas and to tie up bundles of outdated newspapers and magazines for return to the distributor. I also swept and mopped the floors and restocked the candy counters with everything from Clark Bars and Hershey's chocolates to gummy bears and Oh Henry! bars. My dad handled the cigars, cigarettes, and ice cream.

Real boys played baseball, football, and basketball. My interest was in other boys, decorating magazines, and rearranging their mother's furniture.

I surreptitiously hid *House Beautiful* and *Architectural Digest* in my school bag and read them well into the night. I made up decorating projects with imaginary clients and drew up rooms on quarter-inch graph paper.

Around the holidays, Dad's friend Rudy, a professional window dresser, would arrive and create imaginative displays and transform the look of the candy store. He used brightly colored fabrics and props to create levels of display so each gift or toy would stand out, and he highlighted each item with spotlights.

Rudy's talent and technique fascinated me as I observed and absorbed it like a sponge.

When business slowed down and Dad was unable to afford Rudy's design services, I took over and did the displays myself. I experimented with wooden boxes, fishing line, and lighting, using all the tricks that I had learned from Rudy, the master.

When the store was in desperate need of remodeling, Dad decided to add a gift and greeting card section while creating more display space. He called up his friend Kurt, a skilled cabinetmaker who built store fixtures.

I was developing an eye for display, lighting, and design, so I got to help plan the project. I watched in amazement as they took my ideas seriously and implemented most of them. At 13, my confidence was building. At one point I thought, *I can do this, I really can do this.* The store remodel turned out to be a huge success—it was the talk of the neighborhood.

* * *

Brooklyn Tech, an all-boys school, offered drafting and freehand drawing as part of the curriculum. I was ecstatic when we got to architectural drafting and began drawing and conceptualizing houses and buildings.

My aunt Jenny and my aunt Bella both had their houses designed by Pincus Decorators, an upscale furniture company on Flatbush Avenue. To me, their beautifully designed houses were high style and definitely upper class. They had *real* wall-to-wall carpet.

I called Stanley Pincus, the owner, and told him about my passion for decorating and ability to draw floor plans. I told him I'd do anything to work for him and didn't care what he paid me. It was an offer he couldn't refuse, so he hired me.

I vacuumed, dusted, and polished furniture; I helped install draperies and slipcovers and did pickups and deliveries, all the while listening and learning every aspect of the home decorating business. The people on the sales force saw my interest and aptitude for decorating and took me under their wing. They taught me about fabrics, furniture styles, wood finishes, draperies, and slipcovers. I was so eager and personable that they put me on the sales floor as a trainee.

One evening when business was slow, Gussie, one of the leading saleswomen, said to me, "Ken, why don't you take this one," as a elderly bowlegged woman entered the store. So I approached the customer and said, "May I help you, madam?" She responded in a heavy Yiddish accent, "Sonny fella, could ya show me sumting in a cock-table," meaning to say cocktail table.

Gussie, looking and listening intently on how I would handle this customer, started laughing so hard that she spit out the soda she was drinking, ruining a very expensive drapery display next to the sales desk. That was my initiation into furniture sales.

Six months after I walked into Pincus Decorators, I decided this was the path for me. I enrolled in Pratt Institute studying interior design; I continued working for Pincus during the day and attended Pratt at night. After two valuable years at Pincus, I felt it was time to move on and to hit the design scene in Manhattan.

Vanleigh Furniture was looking for a designer to set up and maintain room displays. It was the largest furniture showroom in New York with 67,000 square feet of display space. Furniture was sold off the floor, and new settings had to be created every day. My early training with Rudy came in handy, and my passion for interior design got me the job. Working at Vanleigh and meeting professional architects and interior designers showed me how broad and varied the design world was. I learned how designers spoke to their clients and made presentations, as well as how invaluable pictorial renderings were.

After a year or so at Vanleigh, I was wooed by and started working for a small residential design firm that offered me an opportunity to deal directly with clients. I learned other aspects of the business, from fringes and tassels to lampshades and wallpaper. It was another chance to expand my knowledge and learn about the business end of design.

But my new boss's professional practices were less than scrupulous, and with the creditors nipping at our heels, I decided to check the classified job ads in the *New York Times*. I discovered that Ethan Allen was looking for a store designer. *I can do that*, I thought.

With all my previous knowledge, I was a natural. I landed the happiest job of my career and was traveling all over the United States. Eventually, I settled in Los Angeles, because there were three Ethan Allen stores in California.

In 1967, I started my own interior design firm that grew and ran successfully for 25 years. The original spark came from being repulsed by fake linoleum carpeting and from working with Rudy in Dad's candy store.

The Conversation That Changed My Life

I was thrilled and excited as the sound of Mozart and Beethoven coursed through the earphones of my newly purchased cassette player. I had just arrived in Amsterdam and was looking forward to meeting Stewart in Paris in seven days.

Narrow electric trams clanged busily along the avenues as multitudes of people of all ages were pedaling away on bicycles. Water barges floated easily along the canals as prostitutes poised in their windows in the red-light district waved at onlookers. The Dutch Renaissance buildings with their stepped-gable facades were the backdrop for this living opera that fascinated and delighted me.

Amsterdam, the most liberal city in the world, was to gay life what the Vatican was to the Catholics. We didn't have our own religion, but we had music, opera, the ballet, art, and architecture, and Amsterdam was brimming with them all. My bible for the trip was the newly published *Bob Damron's Address Book*, a gay travel guide. It listed bars, discos, bathhouses, and cruising spots. *Damron's* was all you needed to make connections and friends in most major cities of the world. It was better than belonging to AAA or the Shriners.

The Comeback Inn, a bed-and-breakfast featured in *Damron's*, was located on one of Amsterdam's main canals. I checked in and climbed the steep ladderlike stairs, hauling my luggage up five flights. It was quite a challenge, but I was in great shape at 28 and definitely up to the task.

The Inn's downstairs lounge was furnished with overstuffed Victorian furniture reminiscent of the movie set of *My Fair Lady*. After a full day of traveling and unpacking, I deserved a drink. It was cocktail hour as I entered the lounge; I mingled and gradually made some new acquaintances from Paris, London, and Berlin. After a few glasses of wine and conversation, we decided to go dancing next door at the DOK, the most popular disco in the city. Poppers, or amyl nitrite, were all in vogue. Out went my middle-class inhibitions as the effects of the cocktails and the poppers took over. I don't remember inhaling, but I do remember dancing and having a blast as the disco music reverberated through my body. My torso, feet, and hands seemed to surge through the air in a rhythm all their own.

The next morning we all gathered around a boomerang-shaped breakfast table covered in a brightly flowered oilcloth. Lars—our six-foot-seven chef, built like a linebacker for the Packers and as nelly as RuPaul—cooked and served our breakfast. We laughed and nursed our hangovers as we drank coffee and chattered. He swished from the stove to the breakfast table, vibrating his hips and waving a dishtowel. A few of the guys arrived with their boyfriends from the previous evening amid envious gazes and friendly giggles.

On my third morning at the Inn, Lars poured me some coffee just as a new guy arrived from San Francisco. The new guy, Clyde, mentioned he was an architect, and we struck up a conversation about design and architecture. We talked for quite a while about where we'd been and were planning on going.

"I travel for a year, then work two years, and travel again for a year," Clyde said.

I was fascinated by his unusual lifestyle and the freedom he created for himself.

"How do you manage it?" I asked.

"I work for an architectural office with the understanding that I will be leaving at a certain date. After a year of travel when I'm ready to return, the office hires me back, or I look for another job."

His work model astounded me and left an indelible impression. I had recently started my own design business and was dedicated and felt completely accountable to my clients, but this conversation planted a new seed in my mind: Why not work and schedule my jobs with long periods of time off for travel?

That is exactly what I did. However, it got more complicated when my business grew and I had more employees. But somehow it worked out.

Now, I look back on my life and recall that breakfast conversation at the Comeback Inn and how it changed my life. I could have made a lot more money, but I doubt that it would have been as much fun or as gratifying.

The Gift of Purple

In 1967 the Los Angeles Jewelry Exchange was established in a vintage building on Pershing Square and Hill Street. Terrell and Zimmelman, my new clients, leased the prime space on the seventh floor near the elevators.

Irving Zimmelman and his business partner bought, sold, and traded fine diamonds and estate jewelry. They insisted that we use dark blue as the principal color for their new showroom, as it was best for showing diamonds. After strolling through the building and seeing the other completed spaces, I saw dark blue till I was blue in the face. That's when I made the decision: No blue! I wanted the dominant wall facing the elevators to make a profound statement, so I chose a deep purple-plum wool felt to be laminated on paper and applied to the walls.

When I presented my design, the owners were shocked. They insisted on calling in their wives and the entire sales staff for their input. How could I be so bold as to go out of the norm?

"Ken, we told you that blue was the best color for showing diamonds."

"I know, but let's give the purple a chance. Let's put some diamonds on the fabric and see what you think."

We did, and they had to admit that the diamonds showed up very well against the purple.

"If you don't like it after it's installed, I'll have it removed and replaced at my own expense," I promised.

To make them feel even more comfortable, I suggested using deep blue in the display cases where the actual jewelry would be displayed. They were pleased but kept me to my agreement about the possibility of replacing the laminated purple wool.

The moment the wall covering was installed, the Terrell and Zimmelman showroom became the talk of the jewelry industry. You would have thought I had discovered a new planet! I received several store design awards for it and got publicity in all the trade magazines.

The publicity and success of the Terrell and Zimmelman showroom led me to acquiring numerous store design projects including Scarpe, a high fashion men's shoe boutique on Rodeo Drive in Beverly Hills. The Nunn Bush Shoe Company bought Scarpe, kept the design, and made it their flagship store. The company renamed it The Brass Boot and reproduced the store's design in over 200 locations in malls across America.

Designing a store on Rodeo Drive that went national was a great calling card for me and helped me land many more individual and corporate projects. I credit the rapid success of my design business to my taking a chance and insisting on using the then outrageous color purple.

Good Morning, Mr. Paeper

In 1976 I got a telephone call from Norman Spiegel, a building contractor whom I had worked with on several residential projects.

"Ken, I'm in contact with a man from Holland who is buying a house on Benedict Canyon Road in Beverly Hills next door to José Iturbi, the famous Spanish conductor and pianist. The house was built in the '20s and needs to be gutted, remodeled, and furnished. Are you interested?"

I couldn't get the *yes* out of my mouth fast enough, but I didn't want to sound too hungry either. I told him I'd be delighted.

I met Norman at the house three days later to look it over and scope out the work.

In California in the 1950s, Monterey Spanish architecture took a back seat to modern architecture, and the previous owners had attempted to modernize this architectural gem. The thick stucco walls that had curved arches were squared off with wood paneling. Ugh! The rich hardwood floors were covered with chartreuse shag carpeting. The original Moorish fireplaces were replaced with rectangular black onyx slabs. The theater with its adjacent projection room had heavy, hand-hewn beams that were painted over. Fortunately, they were not removed. The kitchen, which was previously used by staff primarily, had to be relocated and expanded. This would allow for an eat-in kitchen and a breakfast room. Although the old bathroom tiles were charming, we couldn't rescue them. The bathrooms were outdated and had to be gutted and remodeled.

The pool house, pool, and tennis court needed complete updating as well. They were not part of the original house and were added without any design sensitivity. This was going to present a bigger challenge than squared-off arches. Once completed, it would be quite a luxurious home to bring up a family with three teenage boys.

Norman and I talked about the scope of the work and the projected budget. We met one more time to crunch the numbers so we could give the client an idea of the cost and a time frame for completion. The next meeting, in about 10 days, would be with the client. I was a bit nervous and apprehensive because of the size of the project and because it was my first experience working with European clients.

I drove a 1972 bronze Chevy Impala convertible. Most successful interior designers in Los Angeles at the time drove a Mercedes, and some even drove Rolls-Royces. Image was everything! Wanting to impress my prospective client, I rented a black Mercedes 450 SL sedan.

I picked up Mr. Paeper, who was staying at the Beverly Hills Hotel, and we met Norman at the house on Benedict Canyon. Mr. Phillip Paeper was a beautifully, yet casually, dressed angular man in his midforties. He was impeccably groomed and spoke with a brusque, no-nonsense Dutch accent.

We walked through the house as I pointed out all the beautiful details that had been covered over and the possibilities for its restoration.

"Mr. Paeper, I absolutely love the house. It is a classic beauty, and I'd be delighted to work with you on it."

I think he was impressed with me and my attitude, as well as my design expertise. We both seemed to relax a bit as we finished our walk-through and went out to lunch.

As I opened the door to the Mercedes, he turned up his nose and said, "Mister Vite, I hate anything German, especially Mercedes."

Holy shit! I must have turned white and was definitely speechless. I was trying to impress him and instead felt like I had just dropped a turd in the punchbowl.

When we arrived at The Polo Lounge, we ordered drinks, and I leaned over to him and sheepishly said, "Mr. Paeper, I must confess something to you. The Mercedes is not mine. It is rented. I drive a Chevy, but I wanted to impress you and make you feel that you would be dealing with a successful firm."

"Ah! Das ist gut."

He revealed to me that he and his family were imprisoned by the Nazis during World War II. As a young boy, he would play among the piles of dead bodies. His parents were both murdered on Liberation Day. Only he and his sister survived.

I was practically in tears as he confided the story of his past and the terror and loss that he had suffered. I was grateful I had been honest with him about the rented Mercedes. I guess he liked and trusted me enough because I did get the contract.

*   *   *

I met Mrs. Sofia Paeper and the boys, who were still in school, several months after we started the job. When they arrived from Holland, they stayed at the Beverly Hills Hotel in the renowned Bungalow 22. I was impressed.

The only things they brought with them from the Netherlands were antique paintings and four Old Masters in heavily carved frames.

They loved the United States and wanted everything American. Mr. Paeper bought a Pontiac for himself, a Corvette for Mrs. Paeper, and a Chevy Trans AM for Brian, the eldest son. The other boys were not old enough to drive. No Cadillacs or Lincolns for this family—that was too showy and nouveau riche. However, no expense was spared when it came to remodeling and furnishing the house.

We had full crews working on the house, removing the previous remodel and restoring the beautiful arches and plaster details of the '20s. The transformation was exciting and moving along slowly, but the Paepers were patient as long as they saw progress. They appreciated fine materials and workmanship and went along with almost every suggestion.

Sofia was flying back and forth to Europe to be with the younger boys. Brian was enrolled in Beverly Hills High. He wore tight jeans and alligator cowboy boots, very European and high fashion at that time. With his foreign accent and striking good looks, he was a hit with the girls. He would take girlfriends into the pool house, close the door, and steam up the windows. Jimmy, my assistant, and I were distracted by all the action. We were very discreet and cut him a wide berth. We did fantasize about the goings-on in the pool house, however.

I got to meet the Paepers' legendary neighbor, José Iturbi. Unfortunately, it was when he was screaming at the workers jackhammering the pool. To smooth things over, I knocked on his door with an expensive bottle of wine, apologizing for the noise.

*   *   *

The construction phase of the project was coming to a close, and the painters were putting the final coats on the walls. Brian's room, which faced the pool, was done in a butterscotch crème color, with a crisp, white ceiling. At the end of each day, I went around to check the progress. The ceiling color, which was to be white, looked like the wall color.

The next day I talked to the painter and pointed out the error. "Mr. White, the ceiling *is* the color that you specified."

"Well, it looks just like the walls. Please repaint it."

He repainted the ceiling two more times. I was getting frustrated and a bit angry when the painter said, "Mr. White, would you please take off your shades?"

I took off my sunglasses and cringed with embarrassment. My eyeglasses were tinted on top and clear on the bottom. All I could do was laugh out loud and apologize, and I paid him out of my own pocket for all his extra work.

All the new furniture that I had designed and selected was gathered in the warehouse and ready for installation. It took two large moving vans and eight hours to deliver everything. It was my policy to keep the client away from the job on the days of installation. Last-minute adjustments always had to be made. If the clients were allowed to stay, they got in the way, asking questions that distracted us from the job at hand. It also spoiled the excitement of them seeing the completed picture for the first time.

Mr. and Mrs. Paeper showed up once we had finished the installation. I greeted them with champagne and a lovely tray of hors d'oeuvres. I could tell they were pleased and excited as they began calling all their friends to come over to see the house. I left them at around six and turned over the keys.

The next morning, I stopped by to settle up the invoices.

"Good morning, Mr. Paeper, how are you?"

This was my normal greeting, and it elicited his normal response.

"I'm aliyf."

Perhaps this was all the happiness he could muster. I never saw him laugh, tell a joke, or be lighthearted. Apparently, he never fully recovered from the terror he had suffered as a child.

Sofia was the polar opposite. She was a happy, joyful, beautiful woman who spoke with a soft lilt in her lovely voice. She had a twinkle in her eye and a sparkle in her speech even though there was much sadness in her history.

The two younger boys came to America three months later. They loved their rooms and couldn't wait to jump in the pool. All in all, the project was a huge success.

Sex Toys:
The Family Business

"Oye! Only in America," my grandmother would say when presented with a modern invention or something that was out of her old-world, Eastern European sphere of understanding.

She'd be turning in her grave had she read the 2017 article in the *New York Times*, "Making Sex Toys Is a Family Business."

In 1981, a representative of a sex toy manufacturing and distribution company contacted me. They had just leased a store on Hollywood Boulevard and wanted me to design it. My Los Angeles interior design firm specialized in designing retail stores.

On the phone they didn't tell me exactly what the business was but called it an "adult boutique." At the time, LA had several sex shops selling adult toys, marital aids, and fetish-related items. We scheduled a meeting with their Los Angeles representative and the soon-to-be store manager.

A young woman with long auburn hair, tight black jeans, and a stretch tube top voluptuously displaying her ample bosoms arrived at my office with an androgynous-looking younger man. I would later discover that he was the female model in the bondage and restraint section of their catalogue.

After being around the New York and LA gay scene for quite a while, nothing really shocked me, but I was still taken aback. I maintained a professional posture as I looked through the catalogues and discussed the project. Monica, the future store manager, explained that they wanted a modern upscale boutique, in contrast to other seedy sex shops in town. We chatted further about the overall look and the product line, as well as the company's upcoming foray into the retail market. I gave them a time frame for design and construction as well as my fee for the overall project. One week later, we had a signed contract.

At our next meeting, I asked Monica for their catalogue and samples of their products so I could effectively design the fixtures and displays. Two days later, they showed up at my office carrying large cartons packed with dildos, penis extenders, lube, prolonging gel, and items that defied my imagination. It took me a week to wrap my head around it before I could come up with a design concept.

I provided sketches, floor plans, and material boards showing pearl-gray upholstered walls contrasted by chrome and glass moveable fixtures with the latest in track and accent lighting. They loved it, and I proceeded with construction documents and specifications. When they were completed and approved by the client, I put the project out for bid. After releasing the plans to several contractors, I got a call from the president's son.

"My dad just had a heart attack, and I am now running the company until he recovers. Please stop the project," he said. "I never wanted to get into retail in the first place. Now that I'm in charge, we are getting out of our Hollywood lease. We will honor your contract and pay you in full."

I had never met the client, but I was saddened by the unfortunate circumstances. They were a Jewish family from Ohio who started the business in 1976 and would eventually be a major player in what is currently a $15 billion industry.

I was disappointed that my design would never see the light of day. Fortunately, the cartons of dildos and erotica were still in my possession, and the client never requested their return.

As Christmas was approaching, I thought, what perfect gifts the toys would make for my friends. And what a Christmas it was! I instantly became the most sought-after guy at the holiday parties.

My grandmother, may she rest in peace, would be very pleased that I didn't give any away as Chanukah presents.

SundayStyles

The New York Times

Making Sex Toys Is a Family Business

By GUY TREBAY

LOS ANGELES — Back in 1976, when Chad Braverman's father, Ron, invested a small grubstake in a manufacturing start-up, consumers bought his products at the back of seedy bookstores and scurried out with their purchases concealed in brown paper bags.

The younger Mr. Braverman, who was not yet born, grew up ignorant as to how his father made a living. He would be well into his teens before learning that the company his father ran with a partner was not, as he had long supposed, some sort of criminal enterprise.

"It was this big mystery no one ever talked about, what my dad was making," Mr. Braverman, now 35, said recently at the North Hollywood offices of Doc Johnson Enterprises, the family firm. "For a long

The New York Times,
November 19, 2017

GRAHAM WALZER FOR THE NEW YORK TIMES

Silicone casts of pleasure products await inspection at the Doc Johnson plant in the North Hollywood section of Los Angeles.

time I just thought he was in the mafia."

What Ronald A. Braverman did was make rubber penises. He also manufactured latex vaginas and hand-shaped items devised for anal insertion and a variety of other novelties associated with masturbatory pleasures. In the evolving parlance of successive eras, those items were euphemistically known first as marital aids — as though a vibrator were a couples counselor — and then sex toys and, eventually, "pleasure products."

It was still a shadowy niche business when Mr. Braverman founded Doc Johnson, but the company would go on to become the largest producer in what is esti-
CONTINUED ON PAGE 9

That Precious Moment

Mom and Dad sold the Woodhaven candy store in 1966 and moved to Florida. They worked long and hard all their lives and could finally relax in a warm and agreeable climate. I was thrilled and encouraged them to make the move. My sister Marlene, on the other hand, felt abandoned. This puzzled me because she never got along with my mother.

In the winter of 1975, we all decided to have a family get-together and visit the folks in West Palm Beach. I flew in from Los Angeles, while my sister and brother-in-law and the kids came in from New Jersey. A number of my aunts and uncles had already migrated to Florida and lived in the same senior community as my folks.

It was a wonderful reunion with much hugging and kissing and all four aunts squeezing us and pinching our cheeks. I loved the laughter and especially seeing my sister's kids maturing so beautifully. My niece Andrea, whom I adored, was 15, and my nephew Daniel was about 12. He was born soon after I moved to California, so I hadn't had a chance to bond with him as I had with Andrea.

My mother cooked, cleaned, and prepared for weeks before we arrived. She was in heaven. My mother made stuffed cabbage, potato pancakes, and rice pudding, all my favorites. She was a master at ethnic cooking, but simple foods like steak and lamb chops were always cremated. We should have said a blessing for the dead when she brought them out to the table.

On that night, however, the food was perfect. The only thing we all were craving was ice cream. Of course we had to wait the obligatory six hours because, God forbid, we should eat a dairy dessert after a meat meal. Then I remembered that the cabbage was only stuffed with rice and vegetables, so we just had to wait one hour according to Jewish law.

I announced that I was going to The Creamery to pick up some rocky road and pistachio and then took requests from the rest of the family. Daniel jumped at the offer to ride in my Chevy convertible. So off we went. I thought it would be a great opportunity to chat with him and get to know him better.

We got into my rented convertible, and after a brief pause I said, "So, Daniel, how are things going now that you're about to go to high school?"

"Fine," he answered and then told me about the sports he was into and about his friends from grade school and how they were all looking forward to high school.

As we approached The Creamery, Daniel turned to me and said, "Uncle Kenny, can I ask you a personal question?"

"Sure," I said. "You can ask me anything."

I was not prepared for what was to follow. Forty-five different scenarios flashed in my mind, and I started to sweat. Was he going to ask why I left the family in New York and moved to California? Was he going to ask me about growing up with his mom? Was he going to ask me something unknown or hidden about Grandma and Grandpa? My mind was racing.

"Well, ya know, Uncle Kenny, I'm starting to think about girls and things and am starting to have *those* feelings," he said. "What was it like for you?"

I pulled the car over and took a long, deep breath. Actually, I remember several breaths before I answered as tears were forming in my eyes. They came from that tender place within me, as I just witnessed the loving innocence of a child growing and asking the most sensitive of questions.

We sat in the car for what seemed like hours as I responded to all his questions about my life and my lifestyle. His concerns were genuine. He asked about the pain of being gay and different. He feared for my being called names and even harmed. I answered him openly and honestly and as lovingly as the questions were asked.

That precious moment in front of the ice cream store stays with me to this day.

Rising Up to the Truth

Timeworn trucks and minivans lined the dirt driveway as we drove up in my new silver Mercedes.

It was Thanksgiving Day in Ojai, California. My dear friend Jennifer invited me, along with my folks, who had just arrived from New York City, to come out for the holiday celebration.

"Kenneth, what kind of people drive pickup trucks and minivans?" my father whispered with a disapproving tone as we entered the house.

"Oh, Dad, it's 1979, and this is California. People are more relaxed out here. Most of Jennifer's friends are artists," I replied, sensing his concern and discomfort.

I was familiar with Jennifer's free-spirited friends even though they were in sharp contrast to my designer pals in West Hollywood.

Jennifer's newly completed rustic living room with its high-pitched cedar ceiling and huge exposed beams was impressive. The windows faced the back of the wooded property with trails leading to the redwood deck and a huge hot tub where clouds of steam rising out of the water mingled with the puffs of marijuana that hung in the air.

Naked bodies frolicking from the bathroom to the wooden hot tub seemed like a scene from a Fellini movie. Tie-dyed T-shirts, cutoff jeans, and Birkenstocks were the fashion of the day. Jennifer and I had recently returned from India on a spiritual quest, so this type of clothing seemed normal to me.

My mother, on the other hand, was dressed up in flesh-toned nylon stockings, a dove-gray Chanel-styled suit, shiny black leather pumps, and a matching handbag. Dad was wearing a well-tailored sharkskin suit and a heavily starched white dress shirt complete with a red paisley bowtie. They stood out like a priest at a whorehouse.

My folks were troopers and engaged in conversation with Jennifer's folks as we all sat around enjoying the holiday feast. Even I was in shock as naked people traipsed through the living room on their way to the hot tub. I couldn't imagine what was going through my parents' minds.

I didn't have to worry long as my father said to me on our drive back to LA, "Kenneth, who are these friends of yours, and what kind of life are you living in California?" The kicker was, "When are you ever going to get married?"

"Dad, I'm never going to get married, so get off of my back."

The deadening silence in the car that followed was endless. Finally, Dad broke the silence.

"Kenneth, I want to get together with you alone and talk."

We agreed to meet at my office the next day.

Several weeks prior to their arrival, I had completed The Advocate Experience, a two-day workshop educating gay people how to live a life of truth and dignity. I was 39 years old and had been lying to my folks about my sexuality for more than 21 years. The rest of my family, friends, and business associates had known about my lifestyle since I was 18. I was terrified at the prospect of the veil of secrecy being lifted.

Dad entered my office the next day and repeated his question: "Why don't you want to get married?"

I contemplated answering his question and knew I had two options. I could continue the lie with another fabricated story or take a risk and tell the truth.

"Well, Dad, I'm just not attracted to women."

"Oh. Are you attracted to men?"

"Uh . . . yes, I am."

"Oh." Another long pause. "Thank God," he finally said. "At least now I know where you're coming from."

I was amazed and shocked at his reaction. We spent the next two hours unraveling 21 years of lies and stilted conversation. I told him about my life and my friends as I invited him into my world.

"Kenneth, I love you and accept you unconditionally even though I don't understand it," Dad said. "But what happens if you get sick? Who is going to take care of you?"

Suddenly, I felt his deep love and concern as I had never felt before. He asked me if I wanted to tell Mom myself or if I wanted him to talk to her first. I said, "Dad, I would love it if you would tell her—it'd be better if she heard it from you. We could all talk about it later."

That afternoon, I picked them up to go out to lunch. My mother was in the bathroom as my dad greeted me. When she came out to the living room, she was weeping. My mother never wept. She raved, she ranted and screamed, but weeping was not in her repertoire. She came over to me and gently held my face in her hands and kissed me softly as she said, "Why didn't you tell us years ago? Holding that secret must have been terribly painful for you."

I was taken aback by her response. These words were totally out of character for her. I wondered if there was a ventriloquist behind her or if someone else was feeding her the lines.

This opened up hours of conversation regarding her recently discovered gay awareness and sensitivity from watching *The Phil Donahue Show* on TV.

"But Kenneth, you don't look like the others," my mother blurted out.

"No, Mom, I'm not like anyone else, I'm just me."

From then on, our life together was more intimate and genuine than it had ever been.

Coincidently, there was a PFLAG meeting (Parents and Friends of Lesbians and Gays) on Saturday. I asked my parents if they wanted to go to the meeting and meet other families that were dealing with the same issues. They looked at each other quizzically and then said in unison, "We'd love to go."

My 80-year-old parents were among the most vocal of the group as they talked about their love for me and their concerns for my life and my safety.

"It sounds like such a lonely life. We don't understand it even though we love our son."

By the end of the meeting, my folks joined PFLAG and I finally felt that our relationship was now treading on solid ground.

A Night at the Baths

The Everard Baths was a gay bathhouse on West 28th Street in the middle of New York City's wholesale flower market. The baths opened in 1888 in a former church building. Gore Vidal, Rudolf Nureyev, Alfred Lunt, Lorenz Hart, and Truman Capote were among the international clientele who revealed their Everard patronage in their personal writings. The cost was $5 for a locker and $7 for a room; on weekends, the rates were slightly higher.

In the early '60s, the sexual revolution was exploding in both the straight and gay worlds. Bob Dylan and Joan Baez were among the most influential folk singers at the time. Dylan's "The Times They Are A-Changin'" became the activist's theme song, and how apropos it was, especially for me.

I had recently moved out of my parents' home and was living in Brooklyn Heights. Bill Polito, a prominent interior designer and close friend of mine, and I decided to smoke a joint and go to the baths to sow our wild oats. We took the subway and got off at 28th Street, then walked up the street to Everard's. The building was about 75 years old, and the only updates were the exposed fluorescent lights that did little to glamorize the interior. A gruff, hairy cashier scowled at us as he took our money and snarled, "Good evening, gentlemen."

He assigned us to a room and pressed a buzzer to let us in. Signs and arrows directed us to a big-bellied older male attendant. He gave us a towel and a toga, a white cotton sheet with a round hole in the center. We were quite stoned by now and laughed all the way to our room, which was an eight-foot by seven-foot metal cage in the middle of a sea of steel cots. Naked men wearing only togas cruised up and down the halls of plywood cubicles, circling around the rows of cots and our metal cage. Bill and I were horrified at this prisonlike enclosure that the management considered a room. We looked at each other and laughed hysterically.

"This will never do," we said in unison. Bill, using an inflated upper-class English accent said, "Obviously they don't know who we are."

But what could we do?

We were too stoned to go home, so we decided to take the room on as a design adventure.

Downstairs, the attendant distributing the togas and towels accepted our $20 tip, which bought us two huge stacks of cotton togas plus a stack of towels. We could barely carry them all as we made our way up the stairs to rearrange and decorate our soon-to-be palatial salon.

Starting with the metal army cots, we chose a formal face-to-face arrangement. Pillows were borrowed and stolen from everywhere. With them, we created overstuffed formal chaise lounges. The togas became faux-linen draperies with swags and cornices framing the room. We scrounged up lamps and used spittoons as accessories. Chairs and tables were borrowed from the coffee area, along with some reproduction French framed prints.

It was stunning, at least in our heavily drugged eyes. We were so proud of our newly decorated suite that we invited all available men, who howled with laughter and amazement at the swanky fantasy world we had created.

While sobering up on the subway ride home, Bill and I both realized that we had so much fun and laughed so hard that we had forgotten to sow our wild oats.

Some years later, I ran into Bill in front of the Rizzoli Bookstore on Fifth Avenue. We reminisced and chuckled at the innocent and silly times we had during what later was known as the sexual revolution.

Not a shot was fired in this revolution, but it took its toll. Fifteen years later, the AIDS crisis claimed my friend Bill and hundreds of thousands of our brothers and sisters.

Lacy Underwear and Four-Inch Heels

Flaming red hair, Tony Lama boots, a blue denim skirt, a holstered six-gun, plus a tape recorder taped and hidden in my bosom with Ethel Merman belting out, "There's no business like show business."

Wow! What an entrance I am going to make.

Every detail of my costume was in place—except for the wig.

About a week before the big Halloween party, I was having coffee with my friend Richard, explaining my wig dilemma. He also needed a costume and suggested that we both go to Frederick's of Hollywood. Richard told me they specialized in lingerie, clothing, and wigs for kinky women and their husbands who are into lacy underwear and bedroom fantasies.

Richard was built like a longshoreman with broad shoulders, a muscular chest covered in thick black hair, and arms and legs to match. I knew this was going to be fun.

On the way to the wig department, a markdown sign announcing 50 percent off distracted us. Richard was eyeing some skimpy, revealing see-through costumes, but our first priority was to try on wigs.

In my mind, Annie Oakley was either a blonde or a redhead, so I tried on several wigs, but nothing screamed *yes* to me. The only wigs that looked good on me were a black Donna Summer afro and a red Tina Turner shoulder-length number. My fantasy of becoming Annie Oakley from the Wild West was quickly morphing into a Vegas stripper.

We made our way back to the markdown rack, where Richard spotted a merry widow pushup corset that was bright pink satin overlaid with frilly black lace. I found an orange dayglow satin bikini dance hall costume trimmed in black sequins with black tassels at the bosom. It was a kinetic marvel.

Off to the dressing rooms we went, assisted by two young salesgirls watching us in disbelief. As we entered the dressing rooms, other shoppers who were trying on their outfits soon joined us. The sight of two grown hairy men going into the dressing rooms at Frederick's was enough to cause a stir. Trying on our outrageous costumes was a blast. The howls of laughter and the screams of delight from the salesgirls and the other customers brought people in all the way from Hollywood Boulevard.

As we were about to leave the store, I realized I didn't have shoes to go with my new outfit. We put down our packages and started checking out the shoes. I spotted a classic Frederick's backless Spring-o-lator with black patent leather straps across the front, a plywood stacked platform, and a brass and steel stiletto heel. It was a drag queen's fantasy.

A kindly rotund older salesman quickly approached us. He took his leave from a buxom, overly made-up hooker with a pushup bra that held triple-X mega boobs. She was accompanied by her john and had 36 pairs of shoes lined up in a semicircle, trying to make up her mind. The sweating salesman with a wrinkled brow was clearly frustrated and eager to get away from them and wait on us. I pointed to the shoes I wanted. He measured my foot and went into the stock room. He reappeared with several boxes of shoes, apologizing in a heavy Eastern European accent, "I haff da sem exackt shoo mit a strep en da beck." I was disappointed, as I wanted a backless Spring-o-lator, but I tried them on anyway. They fit perfectly. I looked in the slanted floor mirror, did a quick Betty Grable pose with a backward glance, and said, "I'll take them! They are perfect."

The salesman then turned to the hooker and her john and said, "Ya see, dats how ya buys shoos!" Richard and I cracked up laughing while paying the cashier in sheer delight. The fun we had shopping at Frederick's far surpassed the minor giggles we had at our Halloween gala.

You're in the Army Now

The Vietnam War was heating up, and my enlistment number was barely 10 digits away. I had to make a decision: Tell my family and the army my big, dark secret or go for the physical and enlist in a noncombative branch of the armed forces. I was not ready to come out to my folks. So I spread my cheeks and endured the humiliating physical exam.

"Kenny, why don't you go down to the draft board in drag?" my friend Joel suggested. "Many guys I know did it and were handed a deferment."

"Joel, I can't, I just can't, and it's not that easy," I said. "They put you through vigorous psychological tests and even then you don't know. It could create a worse situation."

I was hoping for a 4-F on my physical, but no such luck. Thankfully I found a dental unit that was accepting recruits. It was the least military unit I could join without becoming a conscientious objector. Two weeks later a letter arrived with my orders to report to Fort Dix, New Jersey.

I sublet my apartment for the six months that I'd be away in the army. My parents picked me up to drive me to Fort Dix with my gay secret still intact. There was a mixture of tears as well as relief that I was only going into the reserves.

*   *   *

Basic training was tortuous. Sleeping in the barracks with 50 men in an open area with absolutely no privacy was not the fantasy I was hoping for. It proved to be grueling. I was on the top bunk, and a hot farm boy from Iowa slept below me. I had to consciously keep from staring and drooling. I was frightened, lonely, and going deeper into my self-imposed closet.

"Get down and scrub that floor, ass-wipe, and give me one hundred pushups, you low-life motherfucker," Sergeant Jenkins would shout at us.

Being away from home and everything familiar was hard enough, but having a big, black buck sergeant—whom I secretly desired—yelling and barking orders in the most demeaning way possible put some of us over the edge. The guy in the next bunk cried himself to sleep every night. Then I noticed he was no longer around. I found out that he hung himself in the shower late one night. I was freaking out and scared. I kept thinking, *what if they find out about me?*

* * *

In the latrine, seven toilets were lined up with no partitions in between. I was in shock as naked guys, with their private parts hanging, sat there doing their business while they polished their boots, cleaned their rifles, and shot the shit with each other. The adjacent shower room was a 10-foot by 20-foot area with 12 showerheads lined up on facing walls. A gay guy's fantasy for sure.

Holy shit, what if one of the guys caught me staring and I got a hard-on? I'd be finished.

Luckily, it didn't happen. I was exhausted from the four a.m. forced marches, heavy-duty infantry training, and endless calisthenics. By the end of the eight weeks of basic training, I was worn out but in great shape.

My father beamed as he took a picture of me in my starched khaki uniform. He had it enlarged and prominently displayed it in his candy store. Now I was a *real man* in his eyes. *If he only knew what was brewing below the surface.*

* * *

After basic training, I was sent to San Antonio for medical training. The medical lectures and the battlefield training were horrifying. We learned to bandage wounds, give injections, transport the wounded, and give enemas. The enema training was most mind-blowing. Barracks with 24 metal bunks lined both sides of the barren space where we practiced. We were instructed to fill a stainless-steel irrigating can with warm water after attaching a flexible rubber tube. Half the trainees had to lie on the bed and drop their drawers while the other half inserted the tube in their rectums. The safety clip on the tube was to remain closed. It was hard for me to not check out all the exposed butts, but I reluctantly focused on my own chubby patient.

Then it was my turn to be in bed with my butt exposed. I just lay there when I suddenly felt a rush of warm water entering my body. I yelled, "Stop," but not in time. The safety clip had been released. I must have had a quart of water up my bum as I pulled up my pants and did the hundred-yard dash across the barracks to the latrine. How embarrassing! I was leaking, and they were laughing. Quite a few jokes were exchanged at my expense, but all was soon forgotten.

* * *

I was feeling pretty frisky as I entered the base bowling alley. That's when I met Hector, the good-looking male army nurse. Our gaydar was working as I started a conversation about something mundane. The next thing I knew, we had taken a room at the Gunter Hotel downtown. Hector was tall, well-built, and had a country-boy accent from Arkansas. That's all it took for me to jump his bones and get it on.

The fear that the military police might break the door down and arrest us hung in the air. This was the era of military witch-hunts for gays and other "undesirables." Hector and I had a few more dates before he was sent off to his next duty station in Germany.

Right after Hector left, I landed a cushy job as the company clerk. The job came with a private cadre room at the end of the barracks. My penchant for design and my imagination went into full gear as I set out to create a dream room with no money.

Life magazine had recently published a collection of period paintings from the major museums around the world. I cut out the *Mona Lisa, Whistler's Mother*, van Gogh's *Irises*, plus 10 others. I carefully mounted them on poster board and hung them on the walls to create an art gallery on those otherwise drab gray walls. I borrowed extra footlockers that were stacked in a corner and created banquettes around the room. Using pillows and army blankets I requisitioned from the supply room, I fluffed and puffed and fashioned a chic little seating area. I bought a used radio from an army buddy and I was now ready to entertain, but I couldn't. I was still in the closet. How the guys in my barracks didn't figure out I was gay is still a mystery to me.

One month before completing medical training at Fort Sam Houston, the guys in my barracks and I got a weekend pass. They decided to go across the border to Nuevo Laredo, Mexico, get drunk, and get laid. Countless stories of soldiers going across the border and coming back with the clap (gonorrhea) circulated among the troops. I just wanted to see Mexico.

I piled into one of three cars headed to Mexico, and off we went with my secret still intact. I shared a motel room on the American side of the border with Gary, a guy from Georgia. We called him Spit Shine Gary because his boots were impeccably shined and his rifle and uniforms were always ready for inspection. So was his body. He was a good-looking, muscular Christian guy. He never bragged about his sexual exploits—which was in sharp contrast to the other guys who never stopped talking about theirs.

We arrived at the La Posada Motel, got into our bathing suits, and jumped in the cool turquoise pool. A middle-aged guy sitting under one of the umbrellas started chatting us up and revealed that he was a troubleshooter for Evinrude Motors. The man, Rick, insisted on buying us drinks. Margaritas were only 50 cents, and he kept buying them for us by the dozen. I thought, *What's up with this guy? He looks pretty straight, so why does he keep buying all these drinks for us guys?*

I went along with him when he suggested that we go across to Mexico when the sun went down. I was loaded on the free margaritas and thought that if the hottest man in the world came on to me, I couldn't get it up.

Once we were in Mexico, Rick led us up a potholed dirt road to a nightclub that was right out of *Gunsmoke*. There was a long wooden bar with a mirrored back bar lined with whiskey and liquor bottles. The lighting was dim with enough brightness to see what was going on but not to read a menu or a newspaper. In front of the bar was a huge wooden dance floor with round tables and chairs along the walls, leaving plenty of room for dancing. No one was dancing. Young girls wearing ill-fitting dresses, appearing to be right out of the fields, sashayed around, displaying themselves to the customers.

Rick said, "Ken, that little senorita is checking you out."

I tried to ignore him, but he persisted.

Rick called the girl over and said to her, "You want to fucky with virgin?"

I was dumbstruck. The young girl's eyes lit up. The rest of the guys at our table kept egging me on.

"Go for it, Ken."

The next thing I knew, trying to save face, I gave the bartender the obligatory $2 and took the girl up to a room above the bar. I wondered how Rick knew I was a virgin. Was he just guessing? I'd had sex with men since I was 12 but never with a girl.

At 21, drunk or not, the male physiology took over, and I had full frontal sex with the girl. Afterward, she lovingly cleaned me up with a warm, moist washcloth, and I went into my wallet to give her $20, the going rate at the time.

"Oh no, for love, baby, for love."

She wouldn't take my money.

I was speechless. *All the straight dudes had to pay $20, and the gay guy who couldn't care less got it for free. If they only knew?*

Miracles in My Life

The Puerto Rico travel brochure showed a beautifully furnished room with a balcony overlooking a tropical paradise and the coastline of the Atlantic Ocean.

As I opened the door to this dank and moldy room, I knew I could never stay in this chamber of horrors. Even though it was facing the ocean as promised, it was an assault on my senses. Water-stained and dirt-etched windows, rock-hard beds, and threadbare bedspreads were more than I could bear.

I put on my Speedo, went downstairs, and started walking along the crescent-shaped shoreline, looking for another place to stay. A hotel at the end of the beautiful white sandy beach had throngs of people playing volleyball and basketball in front of it. As I got closer I could see the red tiled roofs, stone arches, gleaming white stucco, and a profusion of bright red and magenta bougainvillea. I was awestruck. The hotel's white concrete sea wall separated the private property from the public beach. I sat on the wall with my back to the ocean and gazed at the vivid colors of tropical plants, the buffed and tanned people at the swimming pool, and the palms swaying to the ocean breeze. I was transported to a lovely dream world, one that was now quite real.

* * *

I was looking, and feeling, pretty good in my Speedo at 21. Suddenly, a middle-aged man, probably in his late forties, approached and introduced himself as Nick.

"Are you staying here?" he asked, nodding to the hotel behind him.

I told him about my moldy room at the hotel down the beach and said I was looking for a new hotel.

"I'm a tour director from Boston and have a group staying at this hotel. Why don't you stay here?" he asked.

"It's way out of my price range," I said. "I am planning on being in San Juan for two weeks."

"How about staying in the cabanas near the pool? They're really inexpensive."

"That would be great. Are there any available?"

In the next moment I was walking with Nick into the lobby of the Condado Beach Hotel. I felt extremely out of place, wearing just a bathing suit and no shirt in such an elegant lobby. But Nick was undaunted. He asked the registration clerk if there were any pool cabanas available.

The clerk said there were none. Nick pressed him a bit, and the clerk said, "Well, Mr. Nicolas, we only have twelve cabanas, and three are reserved for your tour to change in."

Nick was shocked. He had no idea that they had set aside pool cabanas for his party. "Can you give one of them to my friend Ken?" They both agreed and signed some papers. I couldn't believe my luck.

We became great friends straightaway and had dinner and did the clubs for the next few nights. Nick was incredibly bright, charming, and funny. He became a real buddy.

I stayed on for 10 days after he left and had a fun-filled time, even though I missed Nick's companionship and our great time together.

Two weeks later when I was checking out, I looked over the bill. It only totaled $24.10. I said to the clerk, "There must be some mistake."

He looked over the bill and explained to me, "Oh no, Mr. White, you had quite a few phone calls."

The invoice read, "Incidentals only as per Mr. Nicolas." You could have knocked me over with a feather. My two weeks in a first-class hotel, on the beach, in a tropical paradise cost me $24.10. Life was good!

The Right Choice

Soft white snowflakes blanketed the barren trees and covered the dull Brooklyn sidewalk. This familiar scene took on a surreal appearance as I looked out the restaurant window and imagined the long winter ahead. Seven of us were gathered for our end-of-the-week soiree at Junior's Restaurant located right across from the Brooklyn Paramount Theater. I looked over at the historic marquee that once announced appearances of Ray Charles, Dizzy Gillespie, Ella Fitzgerald, and Duke Ellington. The memory of their iconic presence still hung in the air, as did the record-breaking crowds that they attracted.

We were all architecture students from Pratt Institute. Our ages, ranging from 20 to 40, were as diverse as our economic circumstances, gender, and sexual orientation. Gossip and conversation were in full swing as I sat there still looking out the window and dreaming of warmer weather.

"Why don't we all go to Miami or San Juan for a few days?" I said out loud.

The conversation stopped, and continued with Richard saying, "Great, let's do it. My family has a huge house in the Florida Keys. My crazy brother lives there, but he's gone most of the time."

My dream continued with thoughts of warm and sunny Florida weather, plus the fantasy of Richard's family estate and the sparkling turquoise water of our own private swimming pool. But then my practical and responsible side took over. The cost of the flight plus missing work and falling behind in my schoolwork was too much for me to fathom.

The group went to Florida for Thanksgiving, and I stayed home and bore the brunt of the subzero New York winter.

Three weeks later, I met Richard for lunch. I reluctantly asked him how the trip to Florida was, still regretting my overly responsible decision.

"I think you made the right choice," Richard said emphatically. "Katherine and my sister's budding romance didn't last a day. They fought the whole weekend. The weather wasn't all that great either. But the topper happened when we decided to take a dip in the pool. We noticed the pool was covered over with a huge khaki tarp. How incredibly strange! When we pulled back the tarp, we were dumbstruck. The pool was stacked with guns, ammunition, and other military paraphernalia. Turns out my crazy brother was running guns and ammunition to Castro."

I gasped in disbelief as I listened.

"We had planned a relaxing, warm tropical vacation and found ourselves in the middle of an international espionage novella," Richard said, shaking his head. "Standing there in our bathing suits, we had visions of the FBI and the CIA surrounding the estate and arresting all of us. We couldn't wait to get on a plane and away from that house, the stockpile of munitions, and my crazy brother.

"At six on the morning we were packing to leave, we heard police sirens blaring and the roar of a helicopter hovering overhead. 'Oh my God, this is it . . . we're goners!' we were shouting. We were all gathered in the living room, shaking with fear and dreading what might lie ahead.

"As it turned out, there was a drug bust in progress two houses down the street, but we were still worried sick. After what seemed like an eternity, the police and the helicopters finally left, and we were relieved to see that they weren't there for us after all."

After hearing Richard's story, I thanked my lucky stars that I had made the right choice and stayed home.

Pathway to Enlightenment

Disembarking the state-of-the-art British Airways aircraft and facing the chaos of 1979 Bombay and the massive throngs of people were overwhelming. It was like arriving on another planet. Dimly lit bulbs that hung from exposed wires illuminated the dark, dirty, and dusty customs area. There was hardly enough light to read passports or declaration forms.

The connecting flight to Poona was permanently canceled, so the only way for us to get there was a long-distance taxi. After much dialogue and gesturing, we arranged for a taxi leaving the following day.

We found out later that both of Poona Air's aircraft had crashed within the last eight months and there were no plans to replace them. Since the British had left in 1948, India's transportation system left a lot to be desired. Very few trains ran on time, and most vehicles were poorly maintained.

The next morning the taxi arrived with four strangers already stuffed into an old four-passenger subcompact car with no air-conditioning. It reeked of stale perfume, body odor, nicotine, and curry. Our driver, an unusually large, unshaven, unkempt, turbaned man, drove as if he was on speed and it was his very first time at the wheel. He knocked over food stands and street vendors as he sped and careened through the streets. Next to the driver sat a rather well-dressed man in a black suit with a Nehru collar, probably a lawyer. On my left sat a large Indian woman dressed in a red and yellow sari, holding her two-year-old son, who slept or wept through the entire trip. I was wedged between her and a 20-something hippie wearing a colorless, loosely fitting garment that was held in place by a brown leather belt that matched his guitar case.

I was amazed at the hundreds of people mooning us as we left the airport on a newer portion of the roadway. Upon closer observation, I realized they were not mooning us but defecating in an open trench along the road. Ugh!! This began my malodorous tour of India.

As the taxi hurtled from Bombay through the mountain towns and villages, I noticed that cows had the distinct right of way and were adorned with garlands and tassels. All traffic stopped as these revered creatures leisurely passed by. Local villagers lived along the roadside in lean-to huts and cardboard boxes. *Better to be a cow*, I thought. Working-class families lived in mostly unfinished concrete houses, probably without running water. *Can I deal with three months of this?* I wondered. *Where do the expats and the British live?*

The rugged mountainous drive was like an initiation from hell. It was not what I had imagined as the beginning of a spiritual journey, nor did it match the travel agent's colorful and glamorous brochures.

After three and a half hours of torture, we finally arrived in the dusty, sprawling mountain town of Poona. The ancient buildings were burnished over time in shades of red, saffron, and marigold and were adorned with intricately carved latticework, all peeling in the hot August sun. Most of the signage was in Hindi. Rickshaws were the main mode of transportation peddled by young men wearing lungis, a wraparound piece of cotton cloth twisted into a knot at the waist, like a skirt.

As the taxi pulled up in front of the Blue Diamond Hotel, I sighed in relief. The Blue Diamond was Poona's five-star hotel. At best, it would get three stars in the States, but to me it was heaven, especially at $20 a night. The hotel was located just a short walk to the ashram and boasted the best restaurant in town. Now that

I was comfortable with my accommodations, I was eager to see what lay ahead.

Jennifer, my old friend, former therapist, and spiritual mentor, had arrived a day or so earlier and met me in the lobby. I was thrilled to see her and noticed she was already wearing the ashram's loose-fitting cotton garments in saffron and red, all the prescribed colors, an echo of the sun. They truly complemented her red auburn hair, ruddy complexion, and ample figure.

Most devotees lived at the ashram in tents or in simple dwellings. At the Blue Diamond, we had air-conditioning, maid service, and a concierge. My kind of living! I somehow knew that you didn't need to sit in the dirt with the flies and mosquitoes to become enlightened. It was more of an inward journey.

*   *   *

While seated on the ground under a huge banyan tree, 150 devotees listened intently to Bhagwan Shree Rajneesh's evening message. Bhagwan would place his hand on the forehead of a new devotee, which was supposed to transmit his energy. This ceremony was called Shakti. It was rumored to be an amazing and transformative experience. But I felt nothing!

Pictures were taken as we received this major energy zap. The only exchange of energy I felt was when I took out my wallet and paid for the picture. *Is this what enlightenment feels like?* I wondered.

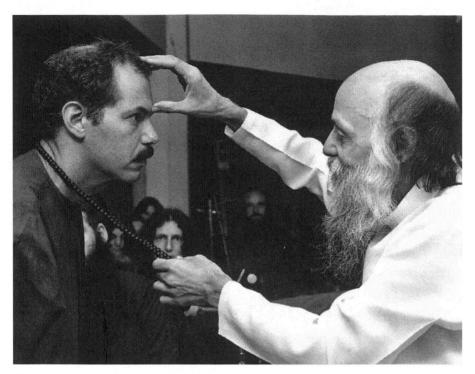

Bhagwan Shree Rajneesh giving me Shakti (an energy transfer).
Later he was known by Osho.

The rest of my time at the ashram and in India was transformative as I discovered my own sense of inner peace and a personal connection to what some people call God or a higher power. I had been on a path of stopping the self-destructive thoughts that were running through my mind and ruining my life—rather than on a path of self-discovery. I knew there was another way to live. People all around me seemed to be having a good time, and that's what I wanted. I wanted to be happy and joyful. Rajneesh and the trip to the ashram was one more step to freeing my mind and my spirit. It also confirmed that I would go to any lengths to find enlightenment or the freedom that it promised.

An eight-day intensive workshop offered at the ashram promised to be transformative. Thirteen countries were represented, with 16 people living together 24 hours a day. Nudity was optional for the workshop. Rajen, the group leader, explained to us that being nude took the sexual charge off of a clothed body so all of our true selves would be revealed.

The nudity actually worked until Rajen, who looked like a pornographic painting of Jesus with ripped muscles and a six-pack, was comforting a young woman from Sweden. She lay across his lap as she was going through a crisis, and all I could see was his already enormous penis growing to its full length and reaching the other side of his thigh. For me, the sexual charge was full-bore as this image was emblazoned into my memory for life.

But the nudity seemed to work during the Truth Circle. We sat around on cushions, facing the leader, and each person was instructed to tell their deepest, darkest secret—something they had never revealed to anyone. The intensity grew as each person revealed the pain, suffering, and shame they were carrying. The humanity and humility that came out of that group might not have been possible without literally stripping naked.

To my left was a pleasant-looking freckle-skinned fellow from Ireland sporting an abundance of thick red hair knotted into a ponytail. We struck up a friendship, as Fred revealed that he was at the ashram with his girlfriend, who decided not to take the intensive workshop. Fred was next in line to share his secret, then it would be my turn. My blood pressure was rising as I was going to reveal that I was gay—and my obsession with the leader and his huge member.

But before I could share my secret, Fred revealed that he was a cross-dresser and loved to go out dancing in full drag. His girlfriend did not have a clue, nor did any of his friends or family. My big secret was no longer a big deal, as Fred was the surprise and focus of the Truth Circle. That evening, the girls in our group provided Fred with clothes and makeup. I did his hair, and we all went out dancing to the nightly music group held in Buddha Hall.

Hearing and seeing a state-of-the-art sound system with huge speakers blasting both Western and Eastern music was overwhelming in contrast to the poverty and the predominance of beggars and lepers lining the streets of Poona. But the music and its volume were mesmerizing. We danced freely and passionately. My conflict was apparent when the dancing included bowing down to Bhagwan Shree Rajneesh. *What the fuck*, I thought, *I am Jewish—we don't bow down to idols or gurus.* I wondered if maybe that was why I didn't feel the power of Shakti. I was a cynic, a Jewish cynic at that. Perhaps I did not open myself up enough. I loved the music. I loved the food. But total devotion to Bhagwan? Not for me.

Rajneesh spoke in English and Hindi on alternate months. At the end of the month when he finished speaking in English, I decided to take a break and spend some time on the beach in Goa before heading north to New Delhi.

*   *   *

My friend and trusted accountant Sid strongly suggested that I visit his guru who was on the outskirts of Old Delhi, in a neighborhood beyond the Red Fort. The taxi dropped me off on a dusty, windswept street that was obviously not the Beverly Hills of India. At the end of the street was a stucco and concrete wall that had weathered many centuries of intense sun, hailstorms, and windstorms. Old worn and battered wooden gates led me into a compound that looked like a ghost town from the Wild West. It was bare of any foliage except for one ancient tree that must have had deep roots, as there was no sign of water anywhere. I was amazed—this was the ashram and spiritual home of Sid's guru?

After the initial shock of the desolate landscape and the grayness of the ashram, a small group of people approached me. They asked if I needed any assistance, and I told them that I was looking to meet with the master. They explained that he was arriving soon and, as the dinner hour was approaching, they invited me to join them. Their kindness, gentleness, and genuine openness was palpable.

The simple meal of curried vegetables, chickpeas, and white rice was delicious. We ate in silence. Later, I was led to the master's house. The evening gathering took place on an enclosed porch with about 15 people present. We sat around on various chairs and couches as the master greeted us all and graciously welcomed me.

He spoke with a calm and benevolence that made me hang onto his every word. What he said, I cannot recall, but I was transfixed and transported to another time. My euphoria was short-lived as he asked me what brought me to India. I was hesitant to reveal that I had come from the Rajneesh ashram as I was warned that Rajneesh's way of thinking was quite controversial. Once my secret was revealed, I got the full blast of what the master thought of Rajneesh and his ashram. I was shocked to learn that in India, Rajneesh was considered a fraud who made a mockery of Eastern belief and the Hindu way of life. I was warned not to wear red and saffron, the Rajneesh colors, while I traveled for fear of scorn or bodily harm. I left the master's house in a state of bewilderment.

*   *   *

I met Jennifer at the train station back in Poona. Her loose-fitting cotton in the colors of the sun were replaced by a white kaftan, and the wooden *mala* with Rajneesh's picture was no longer hanging from her neck.

"We found a new guru," Jennifer announced, "and white is the new color. It stands for wholeness, purity, cleansing, and innocence."

I asked her to tell me more, bewildered at the transformation from red and orange to pure white and from one guru to another.

The new guru and meditation practice took place on the roof-top of our Blue Diamond Hotel. It couldn't have been more convenient. So off we went to downtown Poona and our favorite tailor. We were measured and draped in a flurry of white cotton and silk. Nothing off the rack for us! The garments were all custom made and embarrassingly inexpensive.

The next day, we were dressed in a blaze of snowy-white cotton and stood out like white elephants in a sea of red kaftans and ill-fitting colors of the sun. Undaunted, we began our practice of Kriya yoga with Sadhoji, our handsome new guru with flashing black eyes, on a plush carpet under the stars of India. It was a meditation practice that I had learned 14 years earlier at the Self Realization Center on Sunset Boulevard. Was this a cosmic joke? I had traveled nine thousand miles to experience what was right in my own backyard next door to my favorite Indian restaurant.

Kriya yoga meditation on the roof of the Blue Diamond Hotel
Ken, second from left; Jennifer, second from right;
Sadhogi, new guru, center, in dark robe

Follow Your Dream

In 1989 I saw an ad in *LA Weekly* for a 12-week course in psychic development, so I figured I'd sign up.

The course was given by a well-known TV psychic. Six men and six women, including me, met in her living room the following Thursday. She talked for quite a while about the phenomenon of energy and our innate ability to see, hear, and channel. We split up into groups of two. I was paired off with Jeff, a handsome 45-year-old guy with a great smile.

"Begin by closing your eyes, quieting your mind, and paying attention to your breath," the psychic instructed. "As you sit facing each other, focus on your partner, and just allow thoughts to come. Good. Now, tell your partner what you see or hear, no matter how inane it seems. Don't edit—just let it flow, relax, allow, and speak."

I remember Jeff telling me detailed incidents in my life and predicting happenings in the future, like my upcoming retirement and my leaving LA. Everything he said was spot on.

I clearly recall to this day what I saw and told him.

"I'm seeing an old Moviola machine. I think you're in the motion picture business."

The next visualization I got was a black mortarboard and tassel.

"You're also in education."

Then I saw an old Indian woman seated in front of an adobe house wrapped in a Navajo blanket.

"Jeff, I think you're moving to Mexico."

Suddenly I saw mountains behind the house.

"No, you are moving to New Mexico . . . Santa Fe."

I couldn't believe what was coming out of my mouth, but I kept on going.

"I see a woman on a horse. I think it's your sister. Do you have a sister?"

Jeff revealed to me that he and his sister both taught on an Indian reservation near Santa Fe and she was an avid horsewoman. They met their respective mates, married, and both had two children. While they were teaching, they bought five acres in the mountains above Santa Fe. Their dream was to build two separate houses and live there with their families.

Then Jeff said, "Kenny, I'm also in education. I created and am currently president of the Sony Film Institute, the only private film school in the United States."

Holy shit! I couldn't believe it. It was my first reading, and I was dead on.

After class, Jeff and I went to Jerry's Deli for a bite and talked for hours. He was divorced and had two young daughters he adored. He was HIV positive and had recently broken up with his lover. Jeff and I soon became fast friends. He told me of his declining health and his imminent plan to retire and build on the land in Santa Fe.

I had had a far-off dream to live in Santa Fe as well, but till then, it had been only a dream. I often went there for the opera in July and August and even looked around at real estate. I knew I'd live there someday.

I fell in love with the warm brown adobe architecture, the huge expanses of sky, mountains covered in pinyon pines, and the incredible cloud formations that inspired countless artists like Georgia O'Keeffe, Randall Davey, and Gustave Baumann.

Several weeks later, Jeff and I talked and compared more of our personal stories and the details of our finances. I was in shock when I compared my income with his. I suddenly realized that I could afford to retire and move there as well. His health situation was tenuous, so he had to retire; I just had a dream.

Jeff began designing his house and soon after started construction. I accompanied him on several site visits and got caught up in the excitement. I contacted a realtor I had met on an earlier visit and within a week, I found and bought five acres in the Sangre de Cristo Mountains with a 180-degree view of Santa Fe.

Two years later, I closed my design business, put my house on the market, and made the move, just as Jeff had predicted.

I arrived the Friday before Labor Day in 1991. It was the night of Zozobra, a festival that celebrates the ritual burning of a 50-foot papier-mâché figure of Zozobra, Old Man Gloom, who represents the residents' sadness and gloom. The streets were jam-packed and blocked off with police barricades everywhere. Live bands performed with music blasting through huge loudspeakers. The gargantuan torso of Zozobra was stuffed with all things gloomy—divorce papers, report cards, pink slips, and overdue notices. The elaborate pyrotechnics that burned Old Man Gloom began around nine-thirty at night. Out with the old, in with the new.

I started my two-year practitioner training at the Church of Religious Science a week later, which gave me entre into my new life.

I decided not to build on the land right away; instead, I focused on getting involved in the community. The gods were looking out for me because I bought and fell in love with a house in town and began the remodeling. Even with the unexpected glitches, it was the easiest makeover I'd ever done.

Paul Caron, the contractor, was a dream to work with. He understood my artistic temperament and was not rattled when I made changes. He was tall, good-looking, had a long blond ponytail, blue eyes, and filled out his jeans like a Hollywood porn star. Following him and his bubble-butt up the stairs was a daily treat. I always looked forward to the walk-throughs.

I lived in that house for eight years, my longest and happiest time in any one house. I was retired, had money, a new puppy, and was following my spiritual path. What could be better?

Powwow in Porcupine

Olin West was a man obsessed with Indian lore and the Native American way of life. He was a gifted artist and jewelry maker for the James Reid silversmith shop in Santa Fe and a member of our weekly men's discussion group.

In March of 1995, when Olin announced that he was going to an Indian powwow in Porcupine, South Dakota, my ears perked up and I was immediately intrigued.

"Olin, where the hell is Porcupine, South Dakota, and how far is it from Santa Fe?"

"It's seven hundred and forty miles away. I usually drive it in one day."

"Where do you stay when you're there?"

"Ken, there are no motels close by, so everyone stays in their campers or vans, or they set up a tent or a tepee like I do."

"A tepee? You're kidding, right?"

"No, I'm dead serious."

Reid Austin, another friend from our group, got excited, too. We both decided to rent an RV and go together.

The only available RV within a hundred miles was a 36-foot Winnebago. Neither of us had ever driven an RV much less one of this size. It had a full kitchen, bathroom with a shower, a living room, and a queen-size bed in the rear. It was so big it had three air-conditioning zones. The RV was over the top, but it was all that we could find.

Reid and I picked up our mansion on wheels in Albuquerque on Monday. I nervously drove it home to Santa Fe to stock it with food, duct tape, screwdrivers, a hammer, and a barbecue, getting it ready to leave on Wednesday.

Driving this behemoth on the I-25 felt like maneuvering a ship on wheels. I did most of the driving because Reid was freaking out at the prospect of driving the giant vehicle.

Somewhere in Wyoming along I-25, we spotted Olin driving his Toyota Corolla. Twenty-two-foot tent poles straddled the roof of his car, attached to the front and back bumpers. This tiny car was stuffed with a canvas tepee, gear, luggage, and supplies. What a sight!

Abject poverty is what we encountered as we entered the Dakota Sioux reservation. The houses were unkempt and in disrepair with boarded-up windows and doors. Dirt roads had makeshift signs, if any existed at all. Well-worn pickups and vans were interspersed with individual cars and tents as we entered the hot, dry, and dusty parking area. In the far-off distance, the only other RV we saw was quite a bit smaller than ours. Driving a $150,000 motorhome felt like we were wearing a Gucci tuxedo to a weenie roast. We had our own generator, so landing on this desolate planet seemed feasible, at least for a few days.

Olin found us as we drove up. How could he possibly miss that giant vehicle that could block out the sun.

*   *   *

We followed Olin over to a campsite where guys from all over the country gathered around a roaring campfire with a huge, battered oil drum precariously propped up over it.

"What's in the drum?" I asked.

"It's dinner, and you guys are invited. Take a look."

Huge hunks of beef and fat were floating among potatoes, carrots, and God knows what else. All I saw was a dirty, old oil drum with huge hunks of gray flesh and fat floating in boiling water. The guys gazed at the oil drum as if it were a fine meal that cowhands would eat on the prairie. I nearly threw up looking at it.

"No thanks," I blurted out. "We're having a barbecue, and you guys are sure welcome to join us."

They politely refused our invitation, as I expected.

While preparing our hamburgers of lean top sirloin, I thought we might be viewed as city slickers, driving up in a Rolls-Royce. I wanted to fit in and have a good time, but I would not be eating their grub.

*   *   *

As the sun went down, we heard the beat and pounding of the native drums.

It got louder and louder as we made our way to the drumming circle. Age-old drums of all sizes were pounded upon with leather-bound, hand-hewn wooden sticks. Most drums were simply struck with the heel and palm of the hands. Young boys, teenagers, and men of all ages chanted what seemed like sacred prayers. I could sense the intergenerational pride as the drumming and chanting tradition was passed on from grandfather to son and grandson. I was deeply touched by this prayerful ceremony.

Fifteen minutes later, Olin rounded us up to witness the grand entry parade. The Lakota and the neighboring tribes galloped in on horseback encircling the grass and earthen parade ground as the riders showed off their intricate beadwork, elaborate feathers, and ceremonial dress garments. The deep blues, reds, vibrant indigos, and chrome yellows stood out against their buckskin leggings and dark skin.

Dances were divided into age groups for men and for women. Hand-sewn jingle dresses with hundreds of tiny conical tin ornaments sparkled and tinkled with every movement. Powwow singers and drummers provided rhythm for the dancers using modern speakers and sound equipment.

Spectators were also invited to join some of the dances. Olin dressed me in buckskin leggings, a porcupine quill vest, and a headpiece of rooster feathers sticking straight up from my scalp. I was dressed up and ready for the dance. Who wouldn't be?

I was intimidated as hell but danced anyway. It all seemed curiously familiar as I picked up the beat and the rhythm quite quickly.

*   *   *

Flashing back 17 years to Ojai, California, I remembered a past life regression session. The details of my life as an Onondaga Indian boy living among trees and wildlife came back to me. No wonder the drum circle and the dancing all seemed so exciting and strangely familiar.

*   *   *

As we settled in for the evening, there was a heavy knock on the aluminum door of our Winnebago. When I opened it, six dark-skinned Lakota men with scowls on their faces stood there. I could tell it was not a social call.

"Who are you men, and where are you from?" said the elder in a deep, authoritative voice.

I gave our names and told him that we were friends of Olin West and came to enjoy the powwow.

"Why are you taking so many pictures, and what are you going to do with them?"

Shaking in my boots, I replied, "We've never been to a powwow, and we're admiring the colorful clothing and feathers."

They were not convinced and got into a huddle and talked in their native tongue.

"You are not from the government?" the elder asked me.

"No," I chuckled, "we live in Santa Fe and we're actually anti-government."

"Okay, but no more pictures."

We agreed and took a deep breath as they left our campsite.

The next morning before leaving Porcupine, Olin explained the etiquette of visiting a powwow: pictures are taken only after permission is granted. He also said that many of the feathers on the headdresses and bustles were made from eagle feathers, which are sacred—and protected by the federal government through the 1940 Bald and Golden Eagle Protection Act. Even picking one feather off the ground carried a $5,000 fine or imprisonment. I then realized I could have put the whole tribe at risk.

Fancy feathered bustles of young Native dancers

Awaiting entrance into ceremonial circle

Morocco

The ancient buttresses and whitewashed buildings appeared formidable and alluring as the fog lifted from above the bow. Tangiers was now in full sight. The ferry, loaded with cars, trucks, and passengers, was arriving from Algeciras, a port city in Spain.

It was the year 2000—and my first trip to the intriguing and mysterious continent of Africa.

We disembarked at an industrial dock lined with huge metal warehouses. Local guides dressed in white cotton jellabas hawked their wares and services. The noise seemed to get louder as we headed for the taxis transporting us to the Hotel Continental, just a short distance from the port. Street signs were in Arabic, even though many languages were spoken here; people around me shouted in French, Arabic, and other languages I didn't recognize.

When we arrived at the 19th century Moorish-style hotel, we were greeted by horse-shaped archways, celestial domed ceilings, and a blaze of colorful and intricate tilework. Our guide welcomed us standing in front of an overused school bus. We checked in, dropped our luggage at the front desk, boarded the bus, and were herded into dozens of shops selling Moroccan merchandise. Lemon tea was the bait and lure to sell us rugs, spices, textiles, and locally made brass tchotchkes.

Pushy Moroccan salesmen could win an award for being the most cunning and aggressive in the world. Even I, an expert shopper, overpaid for rugs that I could have gotten cheaper in LA. However, the experience of shopping and bartering in this Berber town was worth every dime. Just knowing I was walking on the same streets as the murderers, spies, foreign diplomats, and writers I'd read about was thrilling.

* * *

The next morning, a private car arrived to take me to Fez and then on to Marrakesh. The olive-skinned, strikingly handsome driver graciously introduced himself as Abdul. He then presented his eight-year-old son, who was a chip off the old good-looking block.

"Mr. Kenneth, this is my son Kadeen. He is the youngest of my five children. I promised him I'd take him along if he did well in his grades. May he come along with us if he sits in the back? He will be very quiet."

I couldn't say no as the boy was adorable, and we had plenty of room in the vintage stretch Mercedes.

As we were leaving Tangiers, we got a flat tire. All businesses were closed because it was Muhammad's birthday. Luckily, there was a roadside tire store and repair shop that was open. We all got out of the hot and dusty car and found some shade as the tire was being repaired. Standing next to the car, I noticed square chrome metal plates with a sizable keyhole on each of the front fenders.

"Abdul, are these plates for a security system?"

"Oh no, Mr. Kenneth, that is where the royal standards are mounted. This was the king's car that I bought many years ago."

Indeed, I was impressed.

We bought Cokes and bottles of water and continued on to Fez with the Atlas Mountains before us. Driving on the road through sand dunes and winding hills, we slowly approached Fez, the country's former cultural capital.

The narrow twisting and meandering cobblestone streets were mesmerizing as we walked into the medina, a medieval walled-in part of the city. The densely populated area of small-scaled buildings dated back to 789 AD. The streets were alive with artisans and food vendors selling their wares. Vividly colored textiles and rugs hung everywhere. Barrels of spices and powdered yarn dye pigments created a tapestry of color that was a feast for the eyes.

I lost sight of Abdul while looking at rugs and sipping lemon tea. He eventually spotted me after 30 minutes of me being lost in the maze while his son was peacefully asleep in the back seat of the limo.

We then went to the mellah, a Jewish cemetery. We made it with an hour to spare. At sundown, it would be closed for the Sabbath. White headstones and elongated igloo-shaped tombs covered the hillside. An ancient white marble slab with wall-mounted faucets was the area for the washing of the hands, a traditional ritual after visiting a gravesite.

I was astonished to learn of the centuries-old Jewish community in Morocco, particularly in Fez, where they were among the first settlers at the end of the eighth century AD. Now there was only a small Jewish presence remaining in Morocco. The enduring cemeteries, synagogues, and buildings stood as a testament to the Jewish influence on the Moroccan culture. You could see Stars of David carved into the sandstone facades as you walked down the ancient streets.

Abdul dropped me at the hotel for an evening on my own. The next morning, his bright eyes welcomed me to the beginning of our lengthy drive along the base of the Atlas Mountains to Marrakesh.

With Kadeen in the back seat reading his schoolbooks, Abdul told me about his wife and five children and the modesty principles and customs of life in Morocco.

"What do you mean you have never seen your wife naked? How did you make five children?" I asked in shock.

"Oh," he said, "I would be too embarrassed to see my wife naked. We use the darkness."

With a flashing gleam in his eye, he said, "Ah, but those American girls!"

With that, he reached under the car seat and pulled out two very worn copies of *Playboy* displaying a nude, amply bosomed Playmate. I was speechless. Abdul went on to explain the many aspects of the Muslim culture that required modesty in a marriage as well as in life in Morocco. A double standard to be sure!

Craggy mountains edged by sweeping sand dunes shepherded us all the way through the mountain roads to Marrakesh. We were greeted by colorful baskets of flowers hanging from light posts along wide, meticulously kept boulevards, as people on bicycles and men in taxis moved along quite effortlessly. Occasionally, camels carrying passengers hugged the right side of the road.

It was dusk as we drove up to L'Orangeraie, an ancient mini-palace known as a riad that had been recently restored and converted into an upscale boutique hotel by a French hotelier. Mosaic-tiled courtyards contained manicured, fruit-laden orange trees. Moorish-arched alcoves revealed lushly upholstered banquettes where men sat around smoking hookahs. Balconies for the harem were now guest rooms facing an interior courtyard. It was the last stop on my trip, so I had decided to indulge myself with some additional luxury.

My room was a two-story suite with a rugged stone staircase that ascended to a private roof terrace overlooking a shimmering turquoise swimming pool. Wow! This was where I was to be served breakfast each morning. The hotel was located within walking distance to the souk and the evening marketplace. I decided to take a stroll and explore the area.

Brightly colored plaster and stone buildings housed shops, cafés, and restaurants that surrounded countless acres of black asphalt. By day it was a parking lot. At sundown, it was transformed into an outdoor marketplace bursting with life. Food carts, displaying beautifully cut meats, sausages, kabobs, and vegetables, appeared everywhere. Seafood of every description, artistically arranged on beds of crushed ice, came rolling in on carts pulled by donkeys. Coffee bars with exotic teas and coffees from around the world and pastry carts with local delicacies suddenly materialized. Wood and metal tables of every size were scattered here and there along with folding chairs and wooden benches. It was like someone said, "Strike that set," and the show began.

I stopped to watch in amazement as a turbaned dentist, who was sitting cross-legged on a folded blanket, nonchalantly extracted an old man's tooth. Adjacent to him was a snake charmer with his flute melodiously enticing a snake from its basket. Captivating aromas of curries and exotic spices mingled with beef and shrimp as portable barbecues and grills sizzled. Chefs and grill masters surrounded by iced tables of produce, meat, and seafood created individual platters as customers delighted in watching them perform their magic.

I joyfully chatted with some locals as I noticed an extremely handsome young man with jet-black flashing eyes in his early 20s following me. I was excited and flattered but had been cautioned against pickups in Morocco. He approached me after I was finishing a conversation and said, "I want to fuck you."

I was taken aback; the fantasy of having sex with this gorgeous man nearly took over my senses.

"I'm sorry, but I can't take you to my hotel," I nervously whispered.

"You can come to my uncle's place. It is very safe."

"I don't think so, but thank you," I said, thinking I'd regret it afterward.

As I agitatedly walked back to my hotel, I thought, *Ken, you might have just dodged a bullet. Who knows what kind of danger you'd be in and what trouble you'd get into in a foreign country?*

* * *

The next evening I walked through the souk clutching my shoulder bag as vendors hawking their goods with bright smiles invited me into their stalls to buy goatskin leather items and all things Moroccan. The sights and aromas of this carnival-like atmosphere were intoxicating. Flashbacks of the previous evening kept coming at me, but my stomach was rumbling even louder. It was time for dinner. After feasting on a steak and shrimp dinner at a grill master's station, I took a walk through the souk on my way back to L'Orangeraie.

The hotel concierge recommended some dependable shops for locally made rugs and textiles for me to visit the next day. The best one was outside the souk in an area where local retail shops catered to upscale clientele. Upon entering the shop, I could see that the quality of the merchandise far surpassed anything I had seen in the souk. The salesman showed me rugs and brassware, silver filigreed candlesticks, and boxes. A camel-bone framed mirror caught my eye, and the bartering began. I loved it. The price was right, but carrying it home seemed arduous.

"We'll pack it with a handle that will make it easy for you to carry," the salesman assured me. "If you don't like the easy-carry package, you don't have to take it."

I was so taken with the mirror that I was willing to give it a shot. As I was paying for my purchases, the salesman leaned over the counter and whispered, "Are you Jewish?"

I was startled by his hushed tone and his question.

"Yes, I am."

Then he said, "It's been such a pleasure dealing with you. We'd like to give you a gift."

He slid open a glass showcase and picked out a large hand-crafted brass mezuzah. He wrapped it and gave it to me, uttering a blessing in Hebrew.

I was taken aback by his kindness and the recognition of a fellow *lantzman*.

The package was easy to carry on the plane, and I was grateful for his persistence and packing expertise. That mirror now hangs in my bedroom as a reminder of Morocco and all the countries I visited, the people I met, and the rich and astonishing experiences I've had in more than six decades of travel.

The Innocence of Youth

The sweet-smelling air tingled my nose with the aroma of wildflowers growing along the ridges and in the fields. Butterflies and insects performed midair as if creating a dance just for me. I was in heaven as I frolicked through the open fields, feeling the golden stalks of grass and dried weeds brush against my sensitive young ankles, knees, and legs.

I had been raised in the noise and traffic of New York City. This new feeling of freedom and openness would influence my life forever.

I walked down the rutted dirt road that was marked by horses' hooves, wagon wheels, and puddles of water left over from the previous night's rain. I spotted some rusty tin cans and wavy pieces of metal that were blown off the roofs of nearby barns— they caught the light of the sun and reflected back radiant reds and copper. I could hear the clucking of chickens and the piercing crows of roosters from over the ridge. "Wake up, wake up," they shouted.

As the rising sun warmed my tender skin and cast long shadows along the ridges and ruts in the road, I felt the joys of freedom and happiness as never before. I stretched out my little arms to capture this wonderful feeling of walking by myself for the very first time in a place of absolute splendor.

For two months my mother, grandmother, aunts, and all us cousins gathered for meals in the kitchen of our white clapboard cottage with the familiar smells of my grandmother's cooking. The men of the family were off working in the city and came up on weekends.

During the day, my mother and aunts would sit on the front porch rocking and chatting while my cousins and I hung around in the shade on the old wooden steps. Occasionally we'd play stoopball, bouncing the soft rubber ball against the steps and trying to catch it. My sister Marlene and cousin Florence's favorite game was potsy, the New York version of hopscotch. After they chalked in the triangular court in the dirt, they'd play for hours. My cousin Robert and I would join in, but the girls were more agile and won most of the games. We were much better at hide-and-seek.

Every other morning as the sun was coming up, the milkman would deliver bottles of cold milk with rich cream floating on the top. We'd save the cardboard stoppers and use them as chips for our card games. We drew straws to determine which cousin got the cool, smooth cream that left a white stain on our upper lips.

On Friday we'd walk along the dirt road to the neighbor's farm to get live chickens and freshly laid eggs. It was fun to see real live chickens and watch as they laid their eggs. The red and black roosters created a lively show for us as they pranced around the fenced-in yard and chased the other chickens that got in their way.

The thought of killing the chickens was pretty gruesome, but we never got to see that actually happen. My grandmother killed the chickens herself to make sure they were fresh and used the chicken feet to add rich flavor to her chicken soup. Unlaid eggs were a delicacy and usually found in those freshly killed chickens. I never liked them.

Horse-drawn wagons were a common sight, and once a month we were treated to a late afternoon hayride that ended up at a farm at the edge of town. We'd laugh, sing, and tell each other jokes as we sat on the bales of hay and chased away the flies. At the end of the ride, there was a clearing in the woods with long wooden tables set with red-and-white checkered tablecloths. A feast of roasted chicken, corn on the cob, homemade coleslaw, and potato salad was waiting for us. Rich and creamy vanilla ice cream was churned by one of the neighbors and heaped onto delicious warm homemade apple pie.

As the sun faded into the horizon, a couple of farmers took out their fiddles and started playing as we clapped our hands and stomped our feet. A base fiddle, accordion, and a harmonica joined in as the grown-ups began dancing and singing to the tunes they all knew.

A square-dance caller showed up, and in no time at all, squares of eight people were formed. The fiddle music started, and the caller, who sounded like an auctioneer, began barking out, "Swing your partner, do-si-do, promenade home" and lots of other instructions that I'd never heard before. I began slapping my hands and stomping my feet with the rest of them. My eyes were as big as saucers as I took in the celebration and fell in love with country music and this simple way of life.

Turning It Over

In 1982 my friends, lovers, and neighbors in West Hollywood were dying of a mysterious disease. It started appearing in 1981 and was spreading like wildfire throughout the gay community. We knew little about what caused it, but it was apparent that it was being transmitted sexually.

The Gay and Lesbian Center in LA had numerous groups that dealt with specific problems in our community. I only qualified for two. I knew I had to get a handle on my sexual behavior because the results were obvious. Having sex and being intimate with multiple partners was like playing Russian roulette. Food was another antidote for dealing with sexual tension, unidentified feelings, and loneliness.

I attended both groups religiously but was like a scared rabbit and didn't speak in the meetings for over six months. Everyone else's stories seemed much more profound and dramatic. I didn't do drugs, I didn't have that much risky sex, I thought, but I was about 25 pounds overweight. I knew I had a problem and decided to deal with it. I kept on going to the meetings and just listened. I learned their often-repeated phrase, "Turn it over, turn it over to God." Well, the only God I knew would not approve of the kind of sex I was having. I kept hearing the phrase repeated over and over and was told that God was not judgmental and was quite loving. I listened and absorbed some of what I was hearing.

After I'd been attending the meetings for six months, I was walking up Highland Avenue toward my car when feelings of rage, anger, frustration, and loneliness coursed through my body. My neck and shoulders were knotted and stiff as a board. I wanted to have sex with the first man in my path and was heading toward the Circle K to eat all its licorice, chocolate, and chewy caramels. I knew I was out of control and the obsessions had taken over.

All of a sudden, I stopped in my tracks, stood still, and said the words that I didn't even believe: "God, I turn this over to you. Please take this from me."

I'll never forget what followed. The rage, anger, and tightness I had experienced moments earlier suddenly left my body. A feeling of deep peace and calm washed over me like a warm shower. I stood in that spot on Highland Avenue, took a deep breath, turned around, walked to my car, and drove home.

From that moment on, I never questioned if God was real or present in my life. I forget sometimes, but I know that *It* is always there. All I have to do is stop, breathe, get quiet, and ask for guidance.

Epiphany

"**Y**ou don't want to grow up to be like your father, do you?" was the daily mantra my mother fed to me until I finally left her house. I don't ever remember her giving me a compliment that wasn't followed by a put-down.

One of the deepest hurts happened when I was about 12 years old. My mother came home from my father's candy store and said, "Mrs. Newman, your teacher, stopped by today to pick up her newspaper. She said what a sweet, bright, and talented young man you are. If she only knew how rotten and ugly you were on the inside, she wouldn't say those things." This and a myriad of other jabs drove me into a lifelong journey of self-examination and psychotherapy.

To my friends, I appeared pretty happy, except for the fact that I had a self-deprecating sense of humor and was constantly second-guessing myself. I was fearful of most people and confrontations, and I hated my mother. I thought this might be normal for a 42-year-old Jewish boy from Brooklyn, yet it plagued me. I was angry and unhappy, and I searched for relief and comfort in every 12-step and self-help program.

In 1982, my friend Joyce asked me to participate in a conjoint therapy session with her therapist. I had never heard of conjoint therapy, and she wouldn't tell me what it was about. She even tried to insist I pay for half the session, but I pushed back. After a little cajoling, she agreed to pay for it, I agreed to join her, and she made the appointment.

Joyce's therapist was Evelyn Silvers, the former wife of actor-comedian Phil Silvers. She was also the first Revlon girl on TV. So, meeting her as a therapist was a bit disarming.

The reason for the session was revealed in our first few minutes together. Joyce, my buddy and confidant, was in love with me even though she knew I was gay. This was not the first time this had happened, but I didn't see it coming.

Evelyn dealt with both of us in the most dignified, understanding, and compassionate way. She asked lots of probing questions and listened intently. I revealed the issues I had with my mother and the pain it caused me. I was in tears by the end of the session.

"Ken, it's obvious you have been deeply wounded as a child and you're still carrying that enormous burden," Evelyn gently told me. "With your permission, we can work on this, and I can re-parent you."

I immediately signed up as a client.

Evelyn did everything she could to build up my self-confidence and even brought me into her inner circle of showbiz clients. Her Thursday evening therapy group was a surreal circle of Who's Who in Hollywood. I still felt like the Jewish kid from Brooklyn dropped into a circle of Hollywood movie stars. George Gobel, the amazing comedian, said it best: "Did you ever feel like the world is a black tuxedo and you were a pair of old brown shoes?" That's how I felt walking into Evelyn Silver's living room for my very first group therapy session.

After two or three gatherings with the Hollywood elite, I felt more at home, even though I still didn't really fit in. They had marriage problems, studio problems, and drug problems. I was still dealing with childhood issues, low self-esteem, and Momma.

Some months later I was sitting in Evelyn's office in a private session when she paused and said, "Ken, tell me about your mother's childhood."

I took a deep breath, stared at the ceiling, and said nothing for what seemed like an awfully long time. I was reviewing what my mother had revealed to me over the years. She talked about her pain and the disappointments she endured as a young immigrant child. But the most indelible memory was when her older brother Morris came back from World War I with dolls and gifts for all her siblings but nothing for her. She repeated this story well into old age.

I started sobbing as tears flowed. Imagining my mother's agony and her lack of love as a child was gut-wrenching. When the rawness subsided, I felt a wave of compassion followed by an upsurge of forgiveness. *She didn't know any better.*

My epiphany came when I realized that she wasn't punishing me intentionally. She was acting out of her own pain and feelings of worthlessness. She didn't know how to love or be loved.

A Heavy Heart

Ghostlike figures slumped over in wheelchairs lined the corridor, some drooling, all with vacant, unresponsive eyes staring into space. My heart sank as I passed these poor souls on the way to visit my sister on her 80th birthday.

The glass and stone entrance surrounded by lush gardens with stalks of purple blooming agapanthus bordered by bright yellow pansies suggested a fine hotel. The sharp contrast of this lovely entrance and what I witnessed in the halls was jarring.

Marlene had multiple sclerosis for 51 years and was now a full-time resident of Daughters of Israel, an upscale nursing home in West Orange, New Jersey. She had been paralyzed for 10 years but had the use of one hand and could speak and think fairly clearly. Her husband, Ted, at 87, had moved in one month after he suffered a fall and could no longer live independently.

The friendly receptionist gave me Marlene's room number and pointed me in her direction. I walked down the hallway and turned the corner past a nurse's station to room 204. Marlene was not there as I had expected, but in an adjacent recreation room seated in a circle with elderly disabled people in wheelchairs. All were attempting to catch a soft plush ball without much success.

I almost didn't recognize her. She was contorted in her wheelchair and appeared to be bloated from steroids or other drugs. This was an alarming difference from my visit nine months before when we were in Marlene and Ted's dining room celebrating Charlie, their eldest grandson, and his new bride.

An attendant wheeled her out to the hallway and turned her over to me as I forced back the tears. I kissed her and held her hand as our eyes met.

"Kenneth, can you believe this," she said, rolling back her eyes as if to say, look at what happens to a person, look at where we wound up.

I choked back the tears. I didn't want her to see my distress and to make her feel worse.

We made our way down the hallway and into an elevator that took us to an unoccupied café on the first floor. The seating area was defined by a wrought iron railing and a hand-painted mural of a charming French café. The area contained three white round tables and six white chairs. Obviously, the chairs were for visiting guests as the residents were either in bed or in wheelchairs. I rolled Marlene in front of the table and sat down next to her.

"Kenneth, it could be worse," she said. "The food is really terrific, and the care I'm getting is exceptional. Teddy got here less than two months ago and has already gained eighteen pounds."

Leave it to my sister to look at the positive side of things, I thought.

"How was your flight?" she asked. "When did you get in? Where are you staying?"

I wanted to talk more about her and how her life had changed in the last few months, but I answered her questions. After she told me about her children and grandchildren, I politely interjected, "Marlene, I brought you some short stories that I've written about the time we were kids growing up behind Dad's candy store."

"Oh, Kenny, that's great, but you'll have to read them to me. My eyes have gotten so bad that I can no longer read regular-sized print."

I took out the collection of stories. I started reading about the joy and excitement we had on Christmas morning and how things changed when we moved to Brooklyn.

We also reminisced about the coldness and aloofness of our European grandmother and her constant criticism of us. We laughed and cried as tears of sadness and joy ran down both our cheeks. We were laughing about our father's wheat germ, black-strap molasses, and cider vinegar diet when Teddy discovered us in the café. I still wanted more one-on-one brother-sister time, but it was just about lunchtime and we were getting hungry.

The three of us were able to have the café all to ourselves as the other residents were attending an outdoor barbecue. An attendant offered us hot dogs and hamburgers. She brought everything in from the barbecue on paper plates heaped with potato salad and coleslaw. I could now see why Teddy gained all that weight.

I began thinking, *it's a Jewish nursing home. The surefire way to keep the troops happy is to have ethnic and comfort food—and lots of it.*

Marlene loved the food too but, more importantly, appreciated the amount of care and attention she was getting, as well as the staff who got her out of bed and into a wheelchair each day.

Teddy, for their entire marriage, wanted to keep her safe and looked after her but in doing so kept her prisoner in their own home. For the last decade, the blinds were kept drawn, and the few visits from friends or relatives were kept to a minimum. Marlene spent most of her life in bed. Their children and grandchildren were not allowed in their home, even to deliver gifts or flowers. All visits were carefully monitored. Marlene was compliant and, I suppose, left with little choice.

A softer version of *What Ever Happened to Baby Jane?* comes to mind.

In hindsight, I think Teddy was suffering from an undiagnosed depression and took my sister along for the ride. His obsession was to keep Marlene safe.

I spent a total of three hours with them at the nursing home. My nephew, Daniel, was right when he said, "Uncle Kenny, that's all the time that you or Mom will be able to handle. She tires easily and needs her rest; you will too."

I wheeled Marlene back to her room, and we sat for a while and looked at the numerous birthday cards and flower arrangements she received. I unwrapped the 10-inch square abstract painting that I made for her in a recent art class, put pushpins into the wall, and hung it where she could see it from her bed. She was ecstatic. Suddenly Marlene's phone rang, and I handed it to her. It was from one of her many friends wishing her a happy birthday.

While she was on the phone, I began recollecting all the trips to see her I had made over the years and our special times together.

* * *

My first plane trip to New York from LA was in the summer of 1970. Marlene took the bus into the Port Authority bus terminal where I met her, and we went to the swanky Palm Court at The Plaza.

"Kenneth, have you seen the prices on the menu?" she asked.

"Yes, but don't worry, I just signed a big project in Texas."

I hadn't just yet, but I didn't want her to be concerned. I wanted her to enjoy our lunch. We each had a glass of chardonnay followed by the coq au vin, which was the special of the day. For dessert we split a spiced pear crumble while we finished catching up on Ted, the children, and family gossip.

There was another time in the early '70s when she met me in Manhattan. This was the day I was planning on coming out to her. We had reservations at a little French bistro on East 58th Street. I ordered an expensive bottle of cabernet sauvignon and an appetizer of duck pâté, an attempt to soften the blow as I tried to get us both plastered. I didn't know that she could drink me under the table. Halfway through the second bottle of wine, I got the courage to tell her that I was gay. She didn't even blink an eye and said, "I knew that, and I still love you. But please don't tell anyone else."

In my mind, her words sounded like "I love you, but I don't want anyone else to know that my brother is a leper." I held that feeling of acceptance yet revulsion for years without questioning her words. Decades later I realized that she wanted to protect me from other people's hurtful prejudice.

As her MS progressed, the options for our little outings became more limited. On one of my later trips, we went to the Short Hills Mall in New Jersey and then to lunch at the Neiman Marcus Café.

We had a great time browsing and chatting, even though it was awkward to talk because Marlene was now in a wheelchair and I was behind her. We strolled past Williams Sonoma, smelled coffee brewing, and decided to drop in. I finally found the coral-colored placemats and napkins that I've been searching for. My sister insisted on buying them for me as a housewarming gift. I treasured them and hated to part with them when they finally faded and frayed over time.

* * *

Christina, a cheerful aide, appeared at the door ready to get Marlene back into bed.

"Hi, beautiful, how was your birthday?" she asked Marlene.

"It was great, thanks." Marlene beamed. "This is my brother Kenny. He came all the way from California to be here for my birthday."

"Ain't that nice," Christina said.

When Christina left, Marlene said, "Isn't she sweet? She's my favorite aide."

Reassured that my sister was in good hands, I kissed her goodbye and walked toward the elevator, passing Teddy's room. He was watching TV as I stopped in to say goodbye.

"Kenny, how do you like the facility? Pretty nice, ha!"

Before I had a chance to answer, he continued, "It's certainly not what I had planned. We hired a round-the-clock live-in caregiver to take care of Marlene because Marcy, who came in five days a week, was just not enough. I moved to the bedroom upstairs so Lori could have the room next to Marlene. Thank God for the electric chairlift that we put in for Marlene. She rarely used it, but I got to depend on it.

"This April I fell out of bed and called Lori for help. She didn't respond. Marlene heard me and called her too, with no answer. I panicked and called the police, who dispatched the fire department. The blast of the sirens from the police and the fire trucks finally woke Lori up. She had taken a sleeping pill and closed her door. We fired her soon after. I then made the decision that we were no longer able to manage by ourselves."

As I looked at the frail 87-year-old man in a wheelchair who had manipulated and controlled my sister's entire married life, the anger I used to feel was replaced by sadness and compassion.

We chatted for a bit more about the incidents that led up to moving to the nursing home before saying goodbye. I asked for his cellphone number and shook his hand, turned toward the door, and left. It was the longest conversation we'd had since my sister first introduced us.

Almost 60 years ago, Ted was a handsome bridegroom walking my sister down the aisle. I was the closeted 17-year-old younger brother who was the self-appointed wedding planner. I knew exactly how things should look. This caused much friction with my new brother-in-law, but I felt it was my job. *Who else could do it*, I thought.

As I sat in the lobby of Daughters of Israel waiting for the taxi to take me back to the hotel, I began daydreaming when I heard the taxi approaching. I took a deep breath, gathered my senses, and walked through the glass doors into a lush world where trees and flowers greeted me but the penetrating sadness lingered.

Marlene and Ted, July 1995

My Sister the Buddhist

Well, she wasn't really a Buddhist, but she seemed to live by many of the Buddhist principles without really knowing what they are.

Marlene was four years older than me. She got married in 1957 as a 21-year-old virgin. She and I awkwardly slept in the same room at our parents' one-bedroom apartment right up to her wedding night. She met Teddy, a principled yet uptight Jewish chemist who eventually would go on to work for the same company for 46 years.

Eight years into their marriage and after the birth of their second child, Marlene was diagnosed with multiple sclerosis and slowly lost her ability to walk, drive, or take care of the children. The doctor and Teddy kept the diagnosis a secret from her, renaming it acute sciatica. Nine years later during a routine checkup, the doctor slipped and said, "So Marlene, how are your MS symptoms?"

In shock, she said, "What MS symptoms?"

I would have sued the doctor and divorced Teddy. But not Marlene; she accepted it and moved on.

*   *   *

Some years later, I said to her, "Marlene, you are amazing. You've had the most challenges in our family, yet you are the most upbeat and positive. How do you do it? Don't you ever get angry or depressed?"

"Yes, of course I do."

"How do you handle it?"

"Well, Kenny, I just think of the alphabet and begin with people's names starting with A for Alice, then Abraham, Archie, and so on. By the time I get to the Cs I forgot what I was upset about."

"You mean to tell me that I've been in therapy for over thirty years, dealing with anger, fear, and depression, and you simply do the ABCs?"

"Yep, it works for me."

My happiest memory of my sister is when we lived behind my father's candy store in Jamaica, Queens. We woke up early one Christmas morning to see what Santa had brought us. The kitchen table was covered in red and green crepe paper and loaded with gifts. We were so excited as we opened our presents: a red fire truck for me with a tall yellow metal ladder and a lifelike rubber doll that cried real tears for Marlene.

That was our last Christmas. My father sold the candy store, and we all moved to Brooklyn to live with our grandparents. That's when I found out that we were actually Jewish. My sister said she knew that all along and was confused when she saw Christmas presents, but somehow at age seven, I never got the message.

I now study Buddhism and can reflect on Marlene's simple wisdom: "All is temporary, and soon it will pass." It seemed to be the way she lived her life.

Teddy, her husband of 61 years, died on May 1, 2018, after a short illness. Even in her grieving, her positive attitude and patience continued as she recalled her last years with him in the nursing home as a honeymoon.

Marlene died peacefully three months later on August 4, 2018.

Baking My First Cake

Plumes of black smoke billowed out from the oven, enveloping my mother's newly painted cloud-pink kitchen. It was not your typical pink. She had chosen it after meticulously testing many samples on the walls. The final choice: a pink resembling soft tufts of cotton candy.

My folks were away for the evening, and my cousin Florence and I, both 11, decided to bake a cake using Pillsbury's angel food cake mix.

Dread and panic took over as I hastily turned off the broiler, grabbed a potholder, snatched the cake pan from the broiler, and threw it into the sink. I turned on the faucet full blast, trying to squelch the smoldering mess. It never occurred to me that the cake was to go in the oven, not the broiler. My mother never used either, and I didn't know the difference.

The oven smoke kept discoloring the vintage white porcelain stove. *Why was it still on fire?* Flames leaped out as I opened the oven door, followed by eye-singeing fumes. Then I remembered: my mother used the oven to store her stash of brown paper bags.

Florence started screaming as I ran to open the window, which was almost impossible to budge from all the years of accumulated paint. The ceiling light fixture and walls were barely visible through the black smoke. I finally opened the window to allow the toxic fumes to escape. As it began to clear, I could see the freshly painted walls streaked with charcoal soot.

Within minutes I heard fire trucks racing up our street with sirens blasting. Evidently a neighbor smelled the fumes and called the fire department. Firemen carrying pickaxes and fire extinguishers pounded on the door to the apartment. After questioning us and determining the danger was over, they left.

"My mother is going to kill us. She just had the kitchen painted!" I yelled.

"Let's try to wash the walls, and maybe she won't notice," Florence suggested.

I knew that wasn't going to work but I thought, *why not give it a try?* We got out a bucket and a sponge mop, took some Spic and Span, and went to town. The beautiful pink walls turned into a charcoal sullied mess with smear marks from floor to ceiling.

"Oh shit, what do we do now?"

It was about six o'clock, and my folks were due back around eight.

"Let's open the windows, air out the apartment, and go for an ice cream," I suggested.

The blessing was that the kitchen was separated from the rest of the apartment by a long hallway. By some miracle, this odd room arrangement worked in our favor as the smoke didn't quite make it down the hall. There would still be hell to pay, and we knew it.

"What the heck happened here?" my mother yelled as they entered the apartment.

"Are you okay?" my father chimed in.

I had visions of my father beating me, though he never did, and my mother yelling at the top of her lungs, which she always did.

But my parents seemed to be more concerned about our well-being than the damage we caused. What a relief! They didn't yell at us or kill us. It was certainly not the ending I had imagined. Florence and I looked at each other and took deep breaths, ever so grateful for their astonishingly calm reaction.

Miss Virgie Lee

At 20, I worked full time in Manhattan, went to Pratt Institute at night, and did small decorating jobs on weekends, while living in a brownstone in Brooklyn Heights. Balancing time for school, work, homework, clients, and cleaning my apartment—plus dealing with my raging hormones—was indeed a challenge.

Vigdor, a new, more mature friend in the neighborhood, had me over for dinner one evening. The subject of time management came up.

"I've got this incredible cleaning lady, Virgie Lee," he boasted. "She only works for single men. She says they are usually at work during the day and she can clean an entire apartment in a flash. The best part is that she only charges five dollars."

"Five dollars?" I couldn't believe it! "Do you think she has some free time?"

My mother never had a maid, but at $5, I was willing to give it a whirl.

I had just signed a new client and had a little extra money, so $5 was nothing, even in those days. I was charging $25 an hour for my services, so the economics of me cleaning my own apartment made absolutely no sense.

I called Virgie Lee the next day, and fortunately she had some time in her schedule. I left an extra key at Vigdor's and scheduled her for every other Tuesday.

When I came home from work, the house sparkled. It even smelled squeaky clean from the Pine-Sol that she used in the bathroom. I was in heaven and living large.

After two years, I still hadn't met her.

I was sick at home one Tuesday when the doorbell rang. My nose was running, and I felt like hell, but I went to the door anyway.

A mature, elegantly dressed black woman stood in my doorway. She wore bright red lipstick, had her hair up in a French twist, and was dressed in a gray man-tailored suit with black alligator heels and a matching handbag.

"Can I help you?" I said.

I thought she was an overdressed social worker who had the wrong apartment.

"Hi, I'm Virgie Lee."

I was dumbstruck. I never knew what she looked like. The vision before me certainly did not fit any mental image of a cleaning lady. I thought to myself, *I should be cleaning for her.*

After the awkwardness of her arrival, she went into the bathroom and came out wearing a starched and pressed white cotton English maid's uniform with crisp ruffles around the neckline, along with sensible white shoes. I went back to bed in disbelief. She went through the apartment like a tornado and left 90 minutes later.

That was over 50 years ago and that lesson in economics still remains with me, as does the pleasure of coming home to a freshly cleaned house.

My Lunch with Maggie

"I can't decide on the sable, the mink, or the silver fox."

Ned said, "Take 'em all."

"But I just can't," murmured my friend Maggie, the new 35-year-old wife of millionaire Ned Doyle.

She grew up in a poor Italian family, always looking for a bargain. Paying retail and making extravagant purchases like three fur coats at one time went totally against her grain. The very next day she went to the Ritz Thrift Store on 57th Street to see if she could find something similar but less expensive. She couldn't help herself; that's how she was brought up.

Ned was a 70-year-old founding partner of Doyle Dane Bernbach, the most prestigious advertising agency in New York City.

I met Maggie at Pratt Institute in an interior design class. She was strikingly handsome with her hair up in a French twist, always wearing oversized gold jewelry that she designed, always fashionably dressed in rich, sumptuous colors. I assumed that her jewelry business was incredibly successful since she drove a new Cadillac Eldorado. I was 19 and very naïve. I later discovered she was being kept by a wealthy Italian furniture maker.

"Kenny, the first marriage was for love; after that, it's money and security," she said emphatically, and meant it.

Two years later she was the winning contender to be the next Mrs. Ned Doyle. Ned had been dating Peggy Cass, the actress, comedienne, and game show panelist. Even though Peggy was an Oscar-nominated actress and Tony Award winner, she was no match for Maggie in the charm and romance department.

On one of my trips to New York, we met at a posh Italian restaurant on East 58th Street. I arrived early, was seated at her favorite table, and was sipping a glass of chardonnay when Maggie arrived. The doors flung open, and you would think a movie star had entered.

"Hello, Mrs. Doyle, so wonderful to see you again, Mrs. Doyle. Your guest has already arrived, Mrs. Doyle."

Everyone turned as she made her entrance, arms open and extended like Auntie Mame, her full-length sable coat brushing the other patrons as she made her way to meet me at her reserved table in the corner.

"Kenny, it is so good to see you." She kissed me on both cheeks.

The waiter then arrived and asked, "The usual, Mrs. Doyle?"

"Si, Gino, I'll have a Bombay gin straight up and a negroni, per favore."

I had never heard of a negroni but was about to learn about it—and a little Italian to boot.

"Have a taste," she said to me. "It's made with gin, Campari, and a little vermouth."

It was served in a short cocktail glass with a twist of orange peel over cracked ice. It looked great, but it was bitter. I was diplomatic, saying, "It's interesting but definitely an acquired taste," as I continued drinking my chardonnay.

"So, Maggie, how does it feel to be Mrs. Ned Doyle?"

"Kenny, I like being married, and the security ain't bad either. Having front row seats at every Broadway show is another perk. But it's still a job and an acquired taste, just like a negroni."

After several rounds of drinks, antipasti, osso buco, a side of gnocchi, plus an assortment of Italian desserts, we were stuffed.

"Why don't you come home with me?" she asked. "You can see the apartment, stay for dinner, and meet Ned."

I began to laugh at the thought of more food but wanted to see their new penthouse apartment.

"I'd love to," I said.

We finished our lunch and made our way out the door to 58th Street. The check never appeared.

"Oh, all this is charged to DDB, Ned's company," she said nonchalantly as we walked to the curb where I thought we would hail a taxi.

A black limo appeared, and a chauffeur got out, opened the passenger door, and said, "Mrs. Doyle, did you enjoy your lunch?"

Wow! I was impressed. Maggie had hit the jackpot.

"Mrs. Doyle, where would you like to go?"

"Let's stop at the butcher on Second Avenue on the way home."

Turning to me, she said, "I'll make veal Milanese with orzo in a pesto sauce, and zucchini with capers. It's Ned's favorite. To tell the truth, I think that's how I got Ned to pop the question. Peggy Cass can't cook."

We pulled up in front of Guido's, where faded gold letters edged in black marked the iconic butcher shop. Maggie, in her full-length fur, 12-carat diamond ring, and Gucci pumps, made her entrance. The old-world butcher shop had sawdust on the floor and a long line of refrigerated showcases with carcasses of pigs, cows, and rabbits hanging above them on steel hooks.

Guido, emerging from behind the refrigerated cases in a blood-splattered apron, shouted, "Mrs. Doyle, buongiorno, it's so good to see you again. How about a song?"

He pulled out two bentwood chairs from the back room and invited us to sit down. He went back again and reappeared with two mandolins.

"This is my friend Kenny from California. What should we play for him?" said Maggie.

I was in awe as I began listening to and watching a scene out of a Verdi opera. They played and sang songs from the small villages of Italy where Guido's and Maggie's parents came from. I had forgotten that she once played the mandolin professionally. Tears of laughter and joy rolled down my cheeks as the singing continued. All this time the chauffeur was circling the block to finally find a much-coveted parking spot in front of the butcher shop.

About an hour and a half later, Maggie said, "Mi amore, I hate to cut this short, but it's almost five o'clock, and Mr. Doyle will be home for dinner. I need two pounds of white veal and twelve spicy sausages."

Our departure from Guido's butcher shop was joyful and tear-provoking, with much hugging and kissing. We got into the limo and headed downtown toward the new penthouse apartment and another Maggie-inspired adventure.

Ernie

My longtime companion lay lifeless in my arms as the doctor dropped the lethal hypodermic needle into the red disposable container. I was numb—time stood still. Screams of pain and anguish reverberated through my body as I shrieked walking down the hallway of the Palm Springs Animal Hospital.

*   *   *

Fifteen years prior, I was schmoozing at a July Fourth barbecue in Santa Fe, New Mexico, where I met Michael and Paul. They were gushing with enthusiasm as they showed me dozens of pictures of their new puppy, Max. I was smitten. Max was the kind of dog I was looking for. He was an 18-pound black-and-white Tibetan terrier with long, floppy ears and soft, shaggy hair.

"Ken, he's playful, good-natured, calm, loves people and kids, doesn't shed, and is easy to train," said Paul.

I was sold. I had recently retired, moved to Santa Fe, and bought a new house with an area for a dog run.

Paul called the dog's breeder in Connecticut. She referred me to Jeanette Chaix, who owned a blue-ribbon kennel in Sebastopol, California. It seemed the planets were aligned. I was planning a trip to visit my friends Mark and Jeff in Santa Rosa, only seven miles from Sebastopol. Jeanette had two litters ready for adoption that would be weaned away from their mommas in two weeks.

My trip to visit Mark and Jeff was filled with excitement and anticipation. I hadn't seen my friends in over a year, and now I'd get to see them and pick up a new puppy as well. They were also dog people and really excited for me.

Mark and I went to the breeder to pick out the puppy. Both of us fell in love with a black-and-white male. Ernie just melted in my arms as soon as I picked him up. He was so calm and docile. Later on, I realized it was all just an act.

He was a hellion for the first two years I had him. Hoping for a transformation, I named him Ernie after Ernest Holmes, the spiritual teacher and founder of the Church of Religious Science. But the dog drove me crazy. He was not easily trainable. I'd sit at the top of the steps and throw the ball down, and he'd run up and down the steps for hours fetching. I couldn't wear him out. Friends told me Ernie was just a puppy and that he'd calm down in a year or two, but I didn't know if I could handle it for a year or two.

Fortunately, I got some good advice and kennel trained him. Ernie would get into his soft-blanketed house, I'd give him a treat, and he'd sleep right through the night. Often, I'd relax in my recliner, and he would curl up and schnoogle with me, lying between my legs, as we would both fall asleep.

We loved to go on summer hikes along the ski trails in the mountains. Occasionally a biker would ride by, and Ernie would run after the bike. Eventually he'd come back, except for the time he didn't. I was panicked and called animal rescue, then my neighbors and friends, and anyone who might have spotted him. The telephone finally rang. "Did you lose a black-and-white dog?"

*   *   *

Winters in Santa Fe were magical. The mountains, hills, and trees were blanketed with clean, soft white snow. I'd buy a cord of wood every winter and had a fire going in the fireplace most evenings. The wood was piled near the entrance to Ernie's dog run. I never dreamed he would climb up the pile of wood and jump over the six-foot coyote fence into the deep ravine below. But that's exactly what he did. Yet another runaway drama.

138

I was at my wits' end. I complained at the pet store to Lois, the Pet-Vet's owner, and asked for her advice.

"Ernie's running away for a reason," Lois told me. "It's hard to read his thoughts. Why don't you call Nancy Goldstein, the animal psychic? My clients have had great success with her."

Why not? My New York friends would laugh me off the planet. But I'd try anything at that point.

Nancy Goldstein was confident we could solve the problem. So I scheduled a telephone appointment.

"Ask Ernie why he is running away," she said.

I thought she was a bit psycho, but I did as instructed.

Then she listened psychically to his response.

"I am so excited about this new world and everything around me. I want to run and play and be free like the birds," was Ernie's response, according to Nancy.

She coached me to tell him, "Ernie, I love you so much, and if you run away, you could get hurt or killed. That would make me so unhappy and hurt me deeply."

To my amazement, Ernie never ran away again.

His boundless energy, willfulness, and not paying attention to simple commands were nevertheless getting to me.

"But Ken, he's only a year old and still a puppy," Nancy would tell me.

* * *

I was leaving on a 10-day trip to New York City and didn't know of a house sitter who would take care of Ernie.

Johnny Mahr, a member of my men's discussion group, owned a kennel about 15 miles out of town. He boasted of a young man on his staff who previously trained guide dogs. I called Johnny and asked to have this young man work with Ernie while I was in New York.

When I came back, I was shocked. The dog I had left was unruly and stubborn. The dog I picked up was mild-mannered and well-behaved. He was happy to see me but obeyed the trainer's command to sit, stay, lie down, and give his paw. He was calm, happy, a pleasure to walk and play with. I was astonished and delighted once the trainer showed me how to work with him and give him commands and rewards.

*　　*　　*

I decided to have a Halloween party at the house with the theme being Spiritual Drag. It sounded like lots of fun, so it was easy to get everyone on board. My friend Larry came as the Dalai Lama in a simple white robe, and Natasha came as Our Lady of Guadalupe dressed in lavender silk with metallic golden rays radiating from the crown on her head. Allan, who was quite obese, dressed as the Borscht Buddha. He wore a brown monk's habit and had a rubber chicken with fresh purple beets and green stalks hanging from a rope around his ample waist. I came as a pregnant nun in a black tunic complete with a starched white wimple. Ernie was dressed in similar drag minus the baby bump. He looked adorable until the guests arrived. He tore off his costume and socialized with the guests. I guess he was too embarrassed to be seen in drag.

*　　*　　*

When we moved to Palm Springs in 2000, Ernie adapted like a trooper. Even the desert heat didn't bother him. Everyone loved Ernie, and he had a whole new family of admirers.

One day I came home after a day of shopping and running errands. Ernie was gone.

I panicked and ran over to the pool where my neighbors were gathered. Bunny was there with her husband, Tony, their adorable three-year-old grandson, and six or eight neighbors.

"Has anyone seen Ernie?" I asked.

"No, we haven't seen him today."

"Oonie, where is Oonie?" Bunny's grandson shouted.

I called animal control to see if he was found or turned in. He wasn't.

Everyone around the pool got dressed and walked or drove around the neighborhood looking for Ernie.

As I drove up and down the streets, I said a prayer. "God, please keep him safe and please bring him home to me."

After returning to my condo an hour later, I glanced at my appointment book. There was an entry at 10 o'clock for the dog groomer. Holy shit! Ernie was at the groomer, and I forgot that I dropped him off that morning. I laughed and cried in relief and ran out to the pool to tell everyone my embarrassing story.

"Okay, everybody, barbecue at my house tonight at five o'clock." I decided to turn this embarrassing incident and humiliation into a fun homecoming event for Ernie.

* * *

A number of years later, at 15, Ernie was having trouble walking on the tile floors and kept slipping and falling into his food. It pained me to see this. Pat, my good friend, said, "Ken, I think it's time to put him down."

I wasn't ready.

"God will tell me when."

Indeed, he did. I came home one day when Ernie was screeching in pain, sitting in his own urine and feces. That was the sign I needed.

I called Pat.

"Would you please come and drive me to the vet? I can't do this alone."

Ernie, 1995

Dressing Up for an Earthquake

On October 1, 1987, at 2:42 a.m., I was tossed out of bed by a 5.9 magnitude earthquake that rocked my house as it swayed like a drunken hooker on six-inch heels. I was shaken and in shock at this ungodly hour. All the earthquake preparedness classes never mentioned cantilevered houses on stilts. The breathtaking views of the Hollywood Sign and Griffith Observatory had sold me on the house. I had briefly considered the safety factor, but the excitement of the view and the low price numbed my intellect.

Positioning myself under a doorway or a solid table (as recommended by traditional earthquake instructions) made no sense as the doorway and the house might also slide down the hill. Getting to safety meant getting out of the house and on to solid ground. I figured that one out all by myself.

I usually sleep in boxer shorts and a T-shirt. The middle of the night in October can be quite chilly in LA, so I rushed into the closet, turned on the light, and grabbed a sweatshirt to put over my T-shirt. Then I went looking for sweatpants that were hanging in a different section of the closet. I selected a pair, put one foot in and then the other as I tried to balance while holding on to the shoe rack that was bolted to the wall. My eyes began to focus as I looked into the full-length mirror. *Holy shit*, I thought, *this will never do*. The pants didn't match or go with the top. So I began searching for a pair of matching or complementary pants.

I donned another pair of sweatpants but was horrified at the colors together. *This is even worse*, I thought.

This crazy shopping spree went on for what felt like 15 minutes. By the time I got out of the house and on to the street, my neighbors were already heading back inside.

Later that day I went to my five o'clock metaphysics class. In an attempt to manage the anxiety we all were feeling, the teacher said, "Let's go around the room and tell what we were experiencing during and after the earthquake."

Jacob started with, "The house was shaking so hard the cupboard doors flew open and the dishes and glasses were falling out and crashing onto the floor. It even broke my grandmother's tea pot."

Rose added, "My dog was shaking, crying, and whimpering and hid under the blankets even after the ground stopped shaking."

Tyler, who was crying, said, "My cat Katie darted out of the house and still hasn't come home."

It was only in the telling of my story and the subsequent laughter that brought me to the realization that my trying on different outfits when the house might be sliding down the hill was pretty bizarre. But to me, at the time, it seemed quite normal.

Made in the USA
San Bernardino, CA
26 June 2020